Select
English Poems

Compiled by
A. Parthasarathy

First	Edition	1995
Second	Edition	2001
Third	Edition	2004
Fourth	Edition	2009
Fifth	Edition	2012

ISBN No: 978-93-81094-06-8

Published by:
A. Parthasarathy
1A Landsend
Mumbai 400 006
India
www.vedantaworld.org

Printed by:
Vakil & Sons Pvt. Ltd.
Industry Manor
Mumbai 400 025
India

CONTENTS

		Page
Preface		5
The Turkey and the Ant	: John Gay	7
The Pond	: Jane Taylor	10
The Olive Tree	: Sabine Baring-Gould	13
Abou Ben Adhem	: James Henry Leigh Hunt	16
Casabianca	: Felicia Hemans	18
The Mountain and the Squirrel	: Ralph Waldo Emerson	21
The Nightingale and Glow-worm	: William Cowper	23
The Pineapple and the Bee	: William Cowper	26
The Toys	: Coventry Patmore	30
The Blind Men and the Elephant	: John Godfrey Saxe	33
The Village Preacher	: Oliver Goldsmith	36
On His Blindness	: John Milton	40

			Page
Even This Shall Pass Away	:	Theodore Tilton	42
The Daffodils	:	William Wordsworth	46
Polonius' Advice in *Hamlet*	:	William Shakespeare	48
Mark Antony's Oration in *Julius Caesar*	:	William Shakespeare	51
Letter to the Earl of Chesterfield	:	Samuel Johnson	61
Laodamia	:	William Wordsworth	64
Andrea del Sarto	:	Robert Browning	73
Sohrab and Rustum	:	Mathew Arnold	86

PREFACE

This work is a selection of some exclusive English poems and literary pieces. Each of them carries a note explaining the meaning and message therein. The note is meant to help you understand the contents of the text. Together they convey great human values. They have been specially selected. Study these values carefully and try to graft them into your personal life.

The three long poems — *Laodamia, Andrea del Sarto, Sohrab and Rustum* — depict the devastating effect of attachment on the human personality. *Laodamia* portrays a woman's attachment for man. *Andrea del Sarto* highlights man's infatuation for woman. *Sohrab and Rustum* shows how parent-son attachment plays havoc in their lives.

Study each poem thoroughly. The overall message in the book should lead you to the deeper philosophy of Vedanta. Vedanta is a system of philosophy which reaches the ultimate experience. It helps you achieve mental peace and bliss as well as success and progress in life. Above all, it ushers you to the goal of Self-realisation. The entire philosophy of Vedanta is presented in two books *The Fall of the Human Intellect* and *The Eternities: Vedanta Treatise* both authored by the compiler of this book.

A. Parthasarathy

THE TURKEY AND
THE ANT

In other men we faults can spy,
And blame the mote that dims their eye,
Each little speck and blemish find,
To our own stronger errors blind.

A Turkey, tir'd of common food,   5
Forsook the barn and sought the wood,
Behind her ran her infant train,
Collecting here and there a grain.
Draw near, my birds, the mother cries,
This hill delicious fare supplies;   10
Behold, the busy negro race,
See, millions blacken all the place!
Fear not. Like me with freedom eat;
An ant is most delightful meat.
How blest, how envy'd were our life,   15
Could we but 'scape the poult'rer's knife!
But man, curst man on turkey preys,
And *Christmas* shortens all our days;
Sometimes with oysters we combine,
Sometimes assist the sav'ry chine.   20
From the low peasant to the lord,
The turkey smoaks on ev'ry board.
Sure men for gluttony are curst,
Of the sev'n deadly sins the worst.
An Ant, who climb'd beyond her reach,   25
Thus answer'd from the neighb'ring beech.
Ere you remark another's sin,
Bid thy own conscience look within.
Control thy more voracious bill,
Nor for a breakfast nations kill.   30

— John Gay

8

Glossary

Line

2	mote	:	a speck, particle of dust
6	forsook	:	abandoned, left
	barn	:	building where grain is stored
7	her infant train	:	her young ones
10	fare	:	food
11	negro race	:	black ants
15	blest	:	blessed
16	'scape	:	escape
	poult'rer	:	one who kills, sells birds
20	chine	:	back-piece of pig
21	low	:	humble
22	smoaks	:	steams
	board	:	dining table
23	curst	:	cursed
24	sev'n deadly sins	:	pride, covetousness, wrath, envy, gluttony, sloth, lechery
26	beech	:	a forest tree
27	ere	:	before
28	bid	:	ask
29	voracious	:	devouring greedily
	bill	:	beak
30	Nor for a breakfast nations kill	:	instead of killing a nation of ants for a breakfast

A turkey lived in a barn with her young ones. She had abundant grain to feed on. But she was not satisfied. She desired a variety in food. So she left the barn to pursue her desire. Soon she found ants. Millions of them. As she feasted on the 'delightful meat' she entertained yet another desire. To escape the butcher's knife. She desired personal security. So does your mind go on desiring. Your desires are endless, insatiable. You can never find contentment through indulgence in your desires. You gain fulfilment only by rising above them. Your intellect must pitch up a higher ideal in life. When you identify with an ideal you rise above the lower desires.

The poem also highlights the human weakness of being extroverted. It is easy to find faults in others. But difficult to recognise your own. Even when your faults are far greater than others'. The turkey was destroying a nation of ants for a breakfast. Unmindful of her grievous act she complains of man killing a turkey for Christmas. The poet draws your attention to your own errors and omissions. Before you point your accusing finger at another, learn to look within. Ensure that you are free from that blemish. Introspect. Analyse your own self. Thus, if each takes care of oneself the world will automatically be taken care of.

The poem cautions humanity against two great impediments to peace and progress in life:

1. The insatiable nature of human desires.

2. The tendency to be extrovert and not introvert.

THE POND

There was a round pond, and a pretty pond too;
About it white daisies and violets grew,
And dark weeping willows, that stood to the ground,
Dipped in their long branches, and shaded it
round.   4

A party of ducks to this pond would repair,
To feast on the green water-weeds that grew there:
Indeed, the assembly would frequently meet
To discuss their affairs in this pleasant retreat.   8

Now the subjects on which they were wont to
converse
I'm sorry I cannot include in verse;
For, though I've oft listened in hopes of
discerning,
I own 'tis a matter that baffles my learning.   12

One day a young chicken that lived thereabout
Stood watching to see the ducks pass in and out,
Now standing tail upward, now diving below:
She thought of all things she should like to do so. 16

So the poor silly chick was determined to try;
She thought 'twas as easy to swim as to fly;
Though her mother had told her she must not go
near,
She foolishly thought there was nothing to fear.   20

"My feet, wings, and feathers, for aught that I see,
As good as the ducks are for swimming," said she;
"Though my beak is pointed, as their beaks are round,
Is that any reason that I should be drowned?"   24

"Why should I not swim, then, as well as a duck?
I think I shall venture, and e'en try my luck!
For," said she — spite of all that her mother had
taught her —
"I'm really remarkably fond of the water."   28

So in this poor ignorant animal flew,
But soon found her dear mother's cautions were
true;
She splashed, and she dashed, and she turned
herself round,
And heartily wished herself safe on the ground.   32

But now 'twas too late to begin to repent;
The harder she struggled the deeper she went,
And when every effort had vainly been tried,
She slowly sunk down to the bottom and died!   36

The ducks, I perceived, began loudly to quack
When they saw the poor fowl floating dead on
its back;
And, by their grave gestures and looks, 'twas
apparent
They discoursed on the sin of not minding a
parent.   40

— Jane Taylor

Glossary

Line

3	weeping willows	:	a species of tree with drooping branches
5	repair	:	go, resort
8	retreat	:	secluded place
9	wont	:	accustomed

11	oft	:	often
	discerning	:	understanding
12	'tis	:	it is
	baffles	:	confuses
18	'twas	:	it was
21	aught	:	anything
26	venture	:	dare to undertake
40	discoursed	:	discussed
	minding	:	heeding

A chick watched the ducks enjoying themselves swimming in a pond. She was obsessed with a desire to swim with them. Her mother warned her not to enter the pond. Unmindful of the warning the foolish chick reasoned to herself, 'my beak is pointed and their beaks are round. Is that any reason why I should be drowned?' Arguing thus she ventured into the water. Soon the poor chick found her mother's cautions true. She struggled in vain, sank to the bottom and died.

The poet draws the parallel to human fallacy. You do not heed scriptural injunction. Your mind is obsessed with desires. Your intellect is at times held hostage by the powerful desires of your mind. The intellect then reasons within the periphery of the mind's desires. In this world people hardly use their intellect or use it to justify what their mind demands. Either way actions are led by the mind's whims and fancies.

It is of prime importance that you develop your intellect. A strong intellect alone can control the mind's desires and direct actions properly. Until then you must seek wise counsel. If you fail to follow either you will expose yourself to the fate of the chick.

THE OLIVE TREE

Said an ancient hermit bending
Half in prayer upon his knee,
'Oil I need for midnight watching,
I desire an olive tree.'   4

Then he took a tender sapling,
Planted it before his cave,
Spread his trembling hands above it,
As his benison he gave.   8

But he thought, the rain it needeth,
That the root may drink and swell;
'God! I pray Thee send Thy showers!'
So a gentle shower fell.   12

'Lord! I ask for beams of summer
Cherishing this little child.'
Then the dripping clouds divided,
And the sun looked down and smiled.   16

'Send it frost to brace its tissues,
O my God!' the hermit cried.
Then the plant was bright and hoary,
But at evensong it died.   20

Went the hermit to a brother
Sitting in his rocky cell:
'Thou an olive tree possessest;
How is this, my brother tell?'   24

'I have planted one and prayed,
Now for sunshine, now for rain;
God hath granted each petition,
Yet my olive tree hath slain!'   28

Said the other, 'I entrusted
To its God my little tree;
He who made knew what it needed
Better than a man like me.   32

Laid I on Him no conditions,
Fixed no ways and means; so I
Wonder not my olive thriveth,
Whilst thy olive tree did die.'   36

— Sabine Baring-Gould

Glossary

Line

8	benison	:	blessing
13	beams of summer	:	sunshine
17	brace	:	strengthen, tone up
19	hoary	:	greyish white with frost
20	evensong	:	evening prayer
27	petition	:	prayer
28	hath slain	:	has killed
35	thriveth	:	thrives

Two hermits planted saplings to grow olive trees. They needed olives to extract oil for their prayer. One of them prayed for rain and sun and frost to cherish his plant. God granted all his prayers but the plant perished. Whereas, the other asked for nothing. He left the plant to God's care. That plant grew into a tree and yielded olives.

So it is with life. If you dictate your will to God. Project your desires upon God. You will gain nothing. Instead perform your obligatory duties and surrender them to God's will. You will then be provided in every way.

The Lord's mysterious power sustains this vast universe. Everything works so meticulously, perfectly. The human intellect cannot conceive how different things and beings orchestrate themselves into the melody of harmonious co-existence in this universe. One ought not to disturb this harmony by one's personal preference and interference with nature. If you choose to assert your individual ego the Lord then hands you the reins of control. You then lose His grace and benevolence. Conversely, when you dissolve your ego and surrender to the total scheme of nature you will receive the Lord's blessing.

ABOU BEN ADHEM

Abou Ben Adhem (may his tribe increase!)
Awoke one night from a deep dream of peace,
And saw, within the moonlight in his room,
Making it rich, and like a lily in bloom,
An Angel writing in a book of gold: 5
Exceeding peace had made Ben Adhem bold,
And to the Presence in the room he said,
"What writest thou?" The Vision raised its head,
And with a look made of all sweet accord
Answered, "The names of those who love the
Lord."   10
"And is mine one?" said Abou. "Nay, not so,"
Replied the Angel. Abou spoke more low,
But cheerily still; and said, *"I pray thee, then,*
Write me as one that loves his fellow-men."

The Angel wrote, and vanished. The next night   15
It came again with a great wakening light,
And showed the names whom love of God had
blessed.
And, lo! Ben Adhem's name led all the rest!

— James Henry Leigh Hunt

Glossary

Line

1	may his tribe increase!	:	may there be more people of Abou Ben Adhem's nature in this world
2	Awoke one night from a deep dream of peace	:	saw in his dream
9	accord	:	harmony
13	cheerily	:	pleasantly
18	lo!	:	behold

In this magnificent poem Leigh Hunt depicts the true aspect of devotion to God, *bhakti*. Abou Ben Adhem, a simple soul, professes no love for God. He only claims that he loves his fellow-men.

Abou dreamt of an angel writing the names of those who loved God. He asked the angel if his name was one of them. The angel replied that it was not so. Abou then requested that his name be written as one who loves his fellow-men. The angel wrote and vanished. The next night it returned with the list of names whom God loved. In that list Abou Ben Adhem's name was foremost.

Devotion to God is therefore directly related to one's love for fellow-beings. God resides in the core of every being. He is the homogenous Conscious-Principle manifesting in the heterogenous variety of beings. To recognise and worship Him in His universal expression is true devotion.

CASABIANCA

The boy stood on the burning deck,
   Whence all but him had fled;
The flame that lit the battle's wreck
   Shone round him o'er the dead.   4

Yet beautiful and bright he stood,
   As born to rule the storm;
A creature of heroic blood,
   A proud though childlike form.   8

The flames rolled on; he would not go
   Without his father's word;
That father, faint in death below,
   His voice no longer heard.   12

He called aloud, *"Say, Father, say,*
   If yet my task be done!"
He knew not that the chieftain lay
   Unconscious of his son.   16

"Speak, Father!" once again he cried,
   "If I may yet be gone!"
And but the booming shots replied,
   And fast the flames rolled on.   20

Upon his brow he felt their breath,
   And in his waving hair,
And looked from that lone post of death
   In still yet brave despair;   24

And shouted but once more aloud,
   "My father! must I stay?"
While o'er him fast, through sail and shroud,
   The wreathing fires made way.   28

They wrapt the ship in splendor wild,
    They caught the flag on high,
And streamed above the gallant child,
    Like banners in the sky.   32

There came a burst of thunder sound;
    The boy, — Oh! where was *he?*
Ask of the winds, that far around
    With fragments strewed the sea,—   36

With mast and helm and pennon fair,
    That well had borne their part,—
But the noblest thing that perished there
    Was that young, faithful heart.   40

— Felicia Hemans

Glossary

Line

Line	Word		Meaning
19	booming	:	roaring, thundering
21	brow	:	forehead
27	o'er	:	over
	shroud	:	wrapping-cloth, covering
28	wreathing	:	encircling, coiling. 'Shroud' & 'wreathing' suggest impending death
29	wrapt	:	wrapped
31	gallant	:	brave, splendid
32	banners	:	flags
36	strewed	:	scattered, spread
37	helm	:	wheel by which rudder is controlled
	pennon	:	flag of ship

The father in the poem asked his son to remain on the ship's deck. He went down to attend to work. While he was engaged in his work below, the ship caught fire. The father perished in the flames. The boy stood on the burning deck. He would not move in deference to his father's instruction. The flames rolled on and consumed him.

The poem may seem to glorify a mere submission by an unintelligent boy. But it carries a deep message. That faith is of vital importance in spiritual practice. The supreme God is unknown. You need a guru (preceptor) to embark on the pursuit of the unknown Reality. Once you have established faith in a guru — father in the poem — you must implicitly follow his instruction. The poet highlights this great quality in a spiritual practitioner.

THE MOUNTAIN AND THE SQUIRREL

The mountain and the squirrel
Had a quarrel;
And the former called the latter "Little Prig."
Bun replied,   4
"You are doubtless very big;
But all sorts of things and weather
Must be taken in together,
To make up a year   8
And a sphere.
And I think it no disgrace
To occupy my place.
If I'm not so large as you,   12
You are not so small as I,
And not half so spry,
I'll not deny you make
A very pretty squirrel track;   16
Talents differ; all is well and wisely put;
If I cannot carry forests on my back,
Neither can you crack a nut."

— Ralph Waldo Emerson

Glossary

Line

3	Prig	:	conceited
4	bun	:	squirrel
9	sphere	:	world
14	spry	:	active, lively

The universe is a composite whole of the animate and the inanimate. Both have distinct roles to play to sustain the world. None more or less important. They serve as spokes in a wheel. God acts as a hub holding them all together. Emerson proclaims this truth. None is superior or inferior to another in the perfectly designed universe. Yet people suffer from complexes of either superiority or inferiority. You must rise above complexes. Dissolve your ego. Just play your role in life to the best of your ability. That leads you to perfection.

THE NIGHTINGALE AND GLOW-WORM

A Nightingale that all day long
Had cheer'd the village with his song,
Nor yet at eve his note suspended,
Nor yet when even tide was ended,
Began to feel as well he might   5
The keen demands of appetite;
When looking eagerly around,
He spied far off upon the ground,
A something shining in the dark,
And knew the glow-worm by his spark,   10
So stooping down from hawthorn top,
He thought to put him in his crop;
The worm aware of his intent,
Harangu'd him thus right eloquent.
　Did you admire my lamp, quoth he,   15
As much as I your minstrelsy,
You would abhor to do me wrong,
As much as I to spoil your song,
For 'twas the self-same power divine,
Taught you to sing, and me to shine,   20
That you with music, I with light,
Might beautify and cheer the night.
The songster heard his short oration,
And warbling out his approbation,
Releas'd him as my story tells,   25
And found a supper somewhere else.
　Hence jarring sectaries may learn,
Their real int'rest to discern:
That brother should not war with brother,
And worry and devour each other,   30
But sing and shine by sweet consent,
'Till life's poor transient night is spent,
Respecting in each other's case
The gifts of nature and of grace.

Those christians best deserve the name 35
Who studiously make peace their aim;
Peace, both the duty and the prize
Of him that creeps and him that flies.

— William Cowper

Glossary

Line

3	eve	:	evening
4	even tide	:	evening
8	spied	:	discovered
10	spark	:	light
11	stooping down	:	swooping, descending
	hawthorn	:	thorny shrub
12	crop	:	mouth
14	harangu'd	:	addressed loud and vehement
15	quoth	:	said
16	minstrelsy	:	music
17	abhor	:	hate
23	oration	:	eloquent speech
24	warbling	:	singing
	approbation	:	approval
27	jarring	:	clashing, quarrelling
	sectaries	:	sects
28	discern	:	judge
32	life's poor transient night	:	through the passage of ignorance-ridden lives
34	grace	:	the blessings of Providence
36	studiously	:	devotedly

The nightingale sings. The glow-worm shines. Together they brighten the darkness of the night. But one night a nightingale spotted a glow-worm and swooped to consume it. The glow-worm, aware of its intent, appealed to the nightingale not to devour it. Instead to join him in entertaining the night — You with music and I with light.

Cowper draws the parallel to life in this world. Humanity is steeped in the darkness of ignorance. Various persons and factions try to entertain the dark passage of human life. Some with music, symbolishing the Path of Devotion, *bhakti*. Others with light, the Path of Knowledge, *gnana*. Thus have several religions sprung to enlighten human beings. The different approaches become necessary to cater to the variety of human personalities. There is no need to antagonise or quarrel with each other. With such understanding all religious factions can strive together to attain Knowledge of the supreme Being.

THE PINEAPPLE AND
THE BEE

The pineapples in triple row,
Were basking hot and all in blow,
A bee of most discerning taste
Perceiv'd the fragrance as he pass'd,
On eager wing the spoiler came,   5
And search'd for crannies in the frame,
Urg'd his attempt on ev'ry side,
To ev'ry pane his trunk applied,
But still in vain, the frame was tight
And only pervious to the light.   10
Thus having wasted half the day,
He trimmed his flight another way.
    Methinks, I said, in thee I find
The sin and madness of mankind;
To joys forbidden man aspires,   15
Consumes his soul with vain desires;
Folly the spring of his pursuit,
And disappointment all the fruit.
While Cynthio ogles as she passes
The nymph between two chariot glasses,   20
She is the pineapple, and he
The silly unsuccessful bee.
The maid who views with pensive air
The show-glass fraught with glitt'ring ware,
Sees watches, bracelets, rings, and lockets,   25
But sighs at thought of empty pockets,
Like thine her appetite is keen,
But ah the cruel glass between!
    Our dear delights are often such,
    Expos'd to view but not to touch;   30
    The sight our foolish heart inflames,
    We long for pineapples in frames,

With hopeless wish one looks and lingers,
One breaks the glass and cuts his fingers,
But they whom truth and wisdom lead,   35
Can gather honey from a weed.

— William Cowper

Glossary

Line

1	triple row	:	three rows
2	all in blow	:	ripe
3	of most discerning taste	:	of distinguished, selective choice – a Dramatic Irony indicating the opposite
6	crannies	:	small openings
8	trunk	:	body
10	pervious to the light	:	transparent
13	methinks	:	I reckon
14	sin and madness of mankind	:	the intellectual poverty and mental agitations of human beings
15	forbidden	:	undeserved
16	vain desires	:	baseless desires
17	spring	:	basis, root
18	fruit	:	result
19	ogles	:	looks amorously
	while Cynthio ogles	:	suggesting the presence of moonlight conducive to amorous indulgences
20	nymph	:	young beautiful maiden
23	with pensive air	:	thoughtful

24	show-glass	:	shop window
	fraught	:	filled
	ware	:	objects for sale
28	cruel glass	:	an example of a Transferred Epithet — cruelty arising from one's frustration is transferred to the glass; also a Pathetic Fallacy — human quality attributed to inanimate glass
29	delights	:	desires
30	touch	:	experience
31	inflames	:	desire kindled
35	truth and wisdom	:	true to own conviction and values

A passing bee perceived pineapples. Arranged in three rows within a glass frame. With eager appetite the bee tried to reach it. It could only see the ripe fruit. But could not get through the glass. Having thus wasted half a day it flew another way.

William Cowper compares the bee's behaviour to that of humanity. He gives two examples to highlight mankind's weaknesses for 'acquisition' and 'enjoyment'. The poet symbolises them as the two cardinal human obsessions for 'wealth' and 'woman'. These weaknesses relate to your physical, emotional and intellectual yearnings. The three rows of pineapple symbolise your attractions at these three levels.

The poet describes a man craving for a woman sitting in a passing chariot. Also a woman who longs for merchandise in show windows. In either case the glass stands between the desirer and the object of desire. The glass indicates the impediments that one faces to fulfil one's desires.

The very sight of a sense-object inflames the mind of the unwise. The mind falls an easy prey to these enchanting sense objects in this world. It develops endless desires. Some people are frustrated all their life unable to fulfil their desires. Others plunge into sense objects rashly and meet severe consequences. Thus people spend half their life in material and sensual pursuit and suffer from disappointment.

The poet concludes beautifully: Those who are truthful and wise find bliss within themselves. They can draw happiness from anything — honey from a weed.

THE TOYS

My little Son, who looked from thoughtful eyes
And moved and spoke in quiet grown-up wise,
Having my law the seventh time disobeyed,
I struck him, and dismissed
With hard words and unkissed,   5
— His Mother, who was patient, being dead.
Then, fearing lest his grief should hinder sleep,
I visited his bed,
But found him slumbering deep,
With darkened eyelids, and their lashes yet   10
From his late sobbing wet.
And I, with moan,
Kissing away his tears, left others of my own;
For, on a table drawn beside his head,
He had put, within his reach,   15
A box of counters and a red-veined stone,
A piece of glass abraded by the beach.
And six or seven shells,
A bottle with bluebells,
And two French copper coins, ranged there with
careful art,   20
To comfort his sad heart.
So when that night I prayed
To God, I wept, and said:
Ah, when at last we lie with trancèd breath,
Not vexing Thee in death,   25
And Thou rememberest of what toys
We made our joys,
How weakly understood
Thy great commanded good,
Then, fatherly not less   30
Than I whom Thou hast moulded from the clay,

Thou'lt leave Thy wrath, and say,
"I will be sorry for their childishness."

— Coventry Patmore

Glossary

Line

Line	Term		Meaning
2	quiet grown-up wise	:	like an adult
6	Mother	:	the capital 'M' suggests the scripture
7	lest	:	for fear of
	hinder	:	prevent
16	counters	:	counting discs used in play
17	abraded	:	worn down
20	French copper coins	:	'French' and 'copper' suggest that the coins are worthless
	ranged	:	arranged
24	trancèd breath	:	sleeplike state indicating death
25	vexing	:	annoying
26	rememberest	:	remembers
29	great commanded good	:	the eternal values of life communicated by preceptors
31	hast	:	has
	moulded from the clay	:	the individuality born out of identification with matter
32	Thou'lt	:	You will
	Thy wrath	:	Your anger
33	childishness	:	pettiness, involvement in the world

The boy in the poem spoke wisely but repeatedly disobeyed his father's instructions. The father struck and sent him to bed. Later he visited the son's room fearing grief might hinder his sleep.

The father found the boy fast asleep. His eyes were still wet from sobbing. And beside his bed he had carefully arranged his simple, trifling playthings. The scene of the child's innocence touched the father's heart. He felt a deep sorrow.

The poet compares the boy's childishness to that of adults. Adults too speak words of wisdom. But they are involved in the petty attractions of this world. People are lost in name, fame, power, position, status, money and family. These are the toys that presently make their joys. A preceptor, signified by 'father', looks sympathetically at their pettiness. Like the father of the boy the preceptor also feels sorry for the childishness of human beings.

THE BLIND MEN AND THE ELEPHANT

It was six men of Indostan
To learning much inclined,
Who went to see the elephant
(Though all of them were blind),
That each by observation
Might satisfy his mind.   6

The First approached the elephant,
And, happening to fall
Against his broad and sturdy side,
At once began to bawl:
"God bless me! but the elephant
Is nothing but a wall!"   12

The Second, feeling of the tusk,
Cried: "Ho! what have we here
So very round and smooth and sharp?
To me 'tis mighty clear
This wonder of an elephant
Is very like a spear!"   18

The Third approached the animal,
And, happening to take
The squirming trunk within his hands,
Thus boldly up and spake:
"I see," quoth he, "the elephant
Is very like a snake!"   24

The Fourth reached out his eager hand,
And felt about the knee:
"What most this wondrous beast is like
Is mighty plain," quoth he;
" 'Tis clear enough the elephant
Is very like a tree!"   30

The Fifth, who chanced to touch the ear,
Said: "E'en the blindest man
Can tell what this resembles most;
Deny the fact who can,
This marvel of an elephant
Is very like a fan!" 36

The Sixth no sooner had begun
About the beast to grope,
Than, seizing on the swinging tail
That fell within his scope,
"I see," quoth he, "the elephant
Is very like a rope!" 42

And so these men of Indostan
Disputed loud and long,
Each in his own opinion
Exceeding stiff and strong,
Though each was partly in the right,
And all were in the wrong! 48

So, oft in theologic wars
The disputants, I ween,
Rail on in utter ignorance
Of what each other mean,
And prate about an elephant
Not one of them has seen! 54

— John Godfrey Saxe

Glossary

Line

1	Indostan	:	India
3	to see the elephant	:	indicates irony
8	happening to fall	:	chanced
10	bawl	:	speak noisily

20	happening	:	chancing
21	squirming	:	twisting
23	quoth	:	said
40	scope	:	reach
46	exceeding stiff and strong	:	obstinate
50	ween	:	think
51	rail	:	scoff, bitterly complain
53	prate	:	to talk foolishly, boastfully

Six blind men went to 'see' an elephant! They described the elephant in their own way. That the elephant was merely a wall, spear, snake, tree, fan, rope. Each certain he was right. Though all were in the wrong. The poet means to draw the parallel to the ignorant who profess to 'know' God.

The elephant is huge. But lack of eyesight prevented the men from knowing it. Similarly, God is infinite. The intellect cannot conceive It. Nor the mind feel It. Nor the body perceive It. The human equipments cannot recognise God. Yet, some are emphatic in their description and explanation of God. The poet cautions humanity against such spiritual blindness. You must rise above fanatic belief and gain true knowledge of God.

THE VILLAGE PREACHER

Near yonder copse, where once the garden smiled,
And still where many a garden flower grows wild;
There, where a few torn shrubs the place disclose,
The village preacher's modest mansion rose.
A man he was to all the country dear,   5
And passing rich with forty pounds a year;
Remote from towns he ran his godly race,
Nor e'er had changed, nor wished to change,
his place;
Unpractised he to fawn, or seek for power,
By doctrines fashioned to the varying hour;   10
Far other aims his heart had learned to prize,
More skilled to raise the wretched than to rise.
His house was known to all the vagrant train,
He chid their wanderings, but relieved their pain;
The long-remembered beggar was his guest,   15
Whose beard descending swept his agèd breast;
The ruined spendthrift, now no longer proud,
Claimed kindred there and had his claims allowed;
The broken soldier, kindly bade to stay,
Sat by his fire and talked the night away;   20
Wept o'er his wounds, or tales of sorrow done,
Shouldered his crutch, and showed how fields
were won.
Pleased with his guests, the good man learned
to glow,
And quite forgot their vices in their woe;
Careless their merits or their faults to scan,   25
His pity gave ere charity began.
Thus to relieve the wretched was his pride,
And even his failings leaned to virtue's side;
But in his duty prompt at every call,
He watched and wept, he prayed and felt, for all. 30
And, as a bird each fond endearment tries

To tempt its new-fledged offspring to the skies,
He tried each art, reproved each dull delay,
Allured to brighter worlds and led the way.

   Beside the bed where parting life was laid,   35
And sorrow, guilt, and pain by turns dismayed,
The reverend champion stood. At his control,
Despair and anguish fled the struggling soul;
Comfort came down the trembling wretch to raise,
And his last faltering accents whispered praise.   40
   At church, with meek and unaffected grace,
His looks adorned the venerable place;
Truth from his lips prevailed with double sway,
And fools, who came to scoff, remained to pray.
The service past, around the pious man,   45
With steady zeal, each honest rustic ran;
Even children followed with endearing wile,
And plucked his gown, to share the good man's smile.
His ready smile a parent's warmth expressed,
Their welfare pleased him and their cares distressed;   50
To them his heart, his love, his griefs were given,
But all his serious thoughts had rest in Heaven.
As some tall cliff that lifts its awful form,
Swells from the vale, and midway leaves the storm,
Though round its breast the rolling clouds are spread,   55
Eternal sunshine settles on its head.

— Oliver Goldsmith

Glossary

Line

1	yonder	:	over there
	copse	:	wooded with small trees
6	passing rich	:	living in comfort
7	ran his godly race	:	directed his divine community

9	to fawn	:	behave servile
13	vagrant train	:	a stream of worthless wanderers
14	chid	:	scolded
18	kindred	:	relation
22	fields	:	battles
25	scan	:	examine
28	failings	:	mistakes
	leaned to virtue's side	:	were beneficial
31	each fond endearment tries	:	very lovingly tries every method
32	new-fledged offspring	:	new-winged young one
33	reproved	:	rebuked, condemned
34	allured to brighter worlds	:	attracted them to higher realms of experience
35	parting life	:	dying person
37	reverend champion stood	:	the preacher's very presence helped, assured
40	accents	:	words
41	unaffected	:	humble
42	adorned	:	decorated
	venerable	:	revered
43	sway	:	influence
44	scoff	:	cavil, slight
46	zeal	:	enthusiasm
	rustic	:	villager
47	wile	:	playful prank
52	serious thoughts had rest in Heaven	:	rooted in the Supreme
53	awful	:	huge, majestic

Oliver Goldsmith's description of the village preacher portrays human perfection. The preacher's personality serves as an ideal for human beings to strive and reach.

The village preacher led a modest and peaceful life. Not enamoured by attractions of the modern world. He was more skilled to raise the poor than to rise himself. Ever dutiful and charitable in nature.

The poet compares the preacher to a bird leading its fledglings from their nest to the open skies. He too allured his fellowbeings to greater and nobler life and himself led the way.

The last few lines contain another beautiful metaphor comparing the preacher to a tall cliff. A cliff rises far above the valley and midway leaves the clouds. All disturbances of rain and storm remain below the level of the mountain's breast. The sun shines eternally on its peak. So too, the preacher's feelings and emotions for others remained with his heart. They never disturbed his serene attunement with the supreme Reality.

ON HIS BLINDNESS

When I consider how my light is spent,
   Ere half my days, in this dark world and wide,
   And that one talent which is death to hide,
   Lodged with me useless, though my soul more bent
To serve therewith my Maker, and present   5
   My true account, lest he returning chide,
   Doth God exact day-labour, light denied,
   I fondly ask; but Patience to prevent
That murmur, soon replies, God doth not need
   Either man's work or his own gifts, who best   10
   Bear his mild yoke, they serve him best, his state
Is kingly. Thousands at his bidding speed
   And post o'er land and ocean without rest:
   They also serve who only stand and wait.

— John Milton

Glossary

Line

	On His Blindness	:	the title indicates Milton's humility, objectivity
1	light	:	life
2	ere	:	before
3	death to hide	:	fatal, terrible to remain without use
4	lodged	:	remaining
	soul more bent	:	inner nature more inclined
6	true account	:	true nature
	lest	:	fearing

	chide	:	rebuke, reproach
7	doth	:	does
	exact	:	extract
8	but Patience to prevent that murmur	:	but with patience the supreme Conscience spoke
9	murmur	:	his earlier complaint
11	mild yoke	:	indicating unegoistic spirit of co-operative work

The title of this sonnet refers to John Milton's own blindness. The poet turned blind halfway through his career. He starts the poem with a complaint: How does God expect me to express my poetic talent without eyesight? However, soon after, he realises that God does not expect anything from anyone. That God, *Brahman* is All-full, free from any want or desire. *Brahman* is like a monarch. Everything functions in His presence but He remains ever-free. They serve Him best who function without ego in a spirit of co-operative endeavour. It is the selfless spirit in action that matters in life. Not what one actually does. So the one who writes poetry and the one who does not — both serve Him. An acknowledgment that speaks of Milton's great humility. The famed last line, 'They also serve who only stand and wait' has been used proverbially ever since.

The sonnet presents two main characteristics of a perfect being — knowledge *(vidya)* and humility *(vinaya)*.

EVEN THIS SHALL PASS AWAY

Once in Persia reigned a king,
Who upon his signet ring
Graved a maxim true and wise,
Which, if held before his eyes,
Gave him counsel at a glance
Fit for every change and chance.
Solemn words, and these are they;
"Even this shall pass away."   8

Trains of camels through the sand
Brought him gems from Samarcand;
Fleets of galleys through the seas
Brought him pearls to match with these;
But he counted not his gain
Treasures of the mine or main;
"What is wealth?" the king would say;
"Even this shall pass away."   16

'Mid the revels of his court,
At the zenith of his sport,
When the palms of all his guests
Burned with clapping at his jests,
He, amid his figs and wine,
Cried, "O loving friends of mine;
Pleasures come, but not to stay;
'Even this shall pass away.' "   24

Lady, fairest ever seen,
Was the bride he crowned his queen.
Pillowed on his marriage bed,
Softly to his soul he said:
"Though no bridegroom ever pressed

Fairer bosom to his breast,
Mortal flesh must come to clay —
Even this shall pass away."   32

Fighting on a furious field,
Once a javelin pierced his shield;
Soldiers, with a loud lament,
Bore him bleeding to his tent.
Groaning from his tortured side,
"Pain is hard to bear," he cried;
"But with patience, day by day,
Even this shall pass away."   40

Towering in the public square,
Twenty cubits in the air,
Rose his statue, carved in stone.
Then the king, disguised, unknown,
Stood before his sculptured name,
Musing meekly: "What is fame?
Fame is but a slow decay;
Even this shall pass away."   48

Struck with palsy, sore and old,
Waiting at the Gates of Gold,
Said he with his dying breath,
"Life is done, but what is Death?"
Then, in answer to the king,
Fell a sunbeam on his ring,
Showing by a heavenly ray,
"Even this shall pass away."   56

— Theodore Tilton

Glossary

Line

2	signet ring	:	a small ring with an impression
3	maxim	:	a principle, pithy statement
5	counsel	:	advice
7	solemn	:	inspiring
9	trains of camels	:	lines of camels
10	Samarcand	:	a city in present-day Afghanistan
11	galleys	:	boats, ships
13	counted not his gain	:	had little value
14	mine	:	referring to land
	main	:	referring to sea
17	'mid	:	amidst
18	zenith	:	height
20	jests	:	entertainments
27	pillowed	:	lying
28	softly to his soul	:	thought within himself
31	come to clay	:	reduce to clay
33	fighting on a furious field	: :	an example of alliteration — a recurrence of the same initial sound in words in close succession
35	lament	:	mourn, wail
41	towering	:	rising high above
42	cubits	:	length of arm from elbow to tip of middle finger, from 18 to 22 inches
	in the air	:	a philosophical implication that fame is futile, insubstantial like air
46	musing meekly	:	reflecting submissively
49	palsy	:	paralysis
50	Gates of Gold	:	entrance to heaven, indicates approaching death

Theodore Tilton presents the king of Persia as a picture of detachment. The king carved a great maxim on his ring: EVEN THIS SHALL PASS AWAY. Rooted in the highest values of life, he lived a life of true renunciation. He would not identify with the best or the worst of things that this world offered him. The king was bountifully blessed with wealth and woman, name and fame. He faced also the pangs of disease, decay and approaching death. But all along he maintained his serenity and objectivity in life.

The world is an admixture of fortune and misfortune, pleasure and pain, virtue and vice. The inevitable pairs of opposites in life are inexhaustible. Your mental equilibrium and intellectual equipoise should remain unaffected by these fluctuations. You become established in that state by your attunement to higher values.

The great king of Persia achieved that exalted state.

THE DAFFODILS

I wandered lonely as a cloud
That floats on high o'er vales and hills,
When all at once I saw a crowd,
A host, of golden daffodils;
Beside the lake, beneath the trees,
Fluttering and dancing in the breeze.   6

Continuous as the stars that shine
And twinkle on the milky way,
They stretched in never-ending line
Along the margin of a bay:
Ten thousand saw I at a glance,
Tossing their heads in sprightly dance.   12

The waves beside them danced; but they
Out-did the sparkling waves in glee:
A poet could not but be gay,
In such a jocund company:
I gazed — and gazed — but little thought
What wealth the show to me had brought: 18

For oft, when on my couch I lie
In vacant or in pensive mood,
They flash upon that inward eye
Which is the bliss of solitude;
And then my heart with pleasure fills,
And dances with the daffodils.   24

— William Wordsworth

Glossary

Line

2 vales   :   valleys

4	host	:	large number
12	sprightly	:	cheerful
14	in glee	:	rejoicing
15	gay	:	happy
16	jocund	:	pleasant
19	couch	:	bed, any place for rest or lying down
20	pensive	:	reflective
22	solitude	:	retreating into oneself

The poem indicates to humanity the path to spiritual Enlightenment. The path encompasses the three disciplines of *karma* (action), *bhakti* (devotion) and *gnana* (knowledge) followed by meditation. Meditation culminates in merger with the supreme Reality.

The first part of the poem deals with action. Wandering alone like a cloud implies selfless service performed in a spirit of detachment. When a spiritual seeker continuously engages himself in service and sacrifice his personality suddenly experiences a unifying feeling of love. The poet very subtly indicates this gush of love by placing a comma after the word 'host'. The joy of love experienced at the sight of daffodils indicates universal love, the essence of devotion. And the words 'gazed and gazed' suggest contemplation and acquisition of knowledge.

The spiritual practice of meditation culminating in Enlightenment is evidenced by the last stanza. The poet's mind is 'vacant' of worldly desire and attachment. He remains 'pensive' in deep thought of Reality. That opens the 'inward eye' referred in the Hindu scriptures as the eye-of-wisdom, *gnana chakshu*. He becomes one with the All. Dances with the daffodils.

POLONIUS' ADVICE IN *HAMLET*

There, — my blessing with thee!
And these few precepts in thy memory
See thou character. Give thy thoughts no tongue,
Nor any unproportion'd thought his act.   60
Be thou familiar, but by no means vulgar.
The friends thou hast, and their adoption tried,
Grapple them to thy soul with hoops of steel;
But do not dull thy palm with entertainment
Of each new-hatch'd, unfledg'd comrade. Beware   65
Of entrance to a quarrel; but, being in,
Bear't that the opposed may beware of thee.
Give every man thine ear, but few thy voice:
Take each man's censure, but reserve thy judgement.
Costly thy habit as thy purse can buy,   70
But not express'd in fancy; rich, not gaudy:
For the apparel oft proclaims the man;
And they in France of the best rank and station
Are most select and generous chief in that.
Neither a borrower nor a lender be: 75
For loan oft loses both itself and friend;
And borrowing dulls the edge of husbandry.
This above all, – to thine own self be true;
And it must follow, as the night the day,
Thou canst not then be false to any man.   80
Farewell: my blessing season this in thee!

— from *Hamlet* by William Shakespeare
Act I, Scene III, Lines 57 - 81

Glossary

Line

58	precepts	:	teachings
	in thy memory	:	remember
59	tongue	:	voice
60	unproportion'd	:	indiscriminate
	his act	:	its act
62	adoption tried	:	their friendship proven
63	grapple them to thy soul with hoops of steel	:	embrace them whole-heartedly
65	new-hatch'd, unfledg'd comrade	:	of chance, unproven friendship
70	habit	:	lifestyle
72	apparel	:	dress
74	chief	:	best
77	husbandry	:	farming, economy
81	season	:	assimilate, to imbue, preserve from decay

This is an extract from Shakespeare's play *Hamlet*. Polonius' invaluable advice to son Leartes on the eve of his departure to study abroad. An advice which will serve as life's guidelines to all humanity:

Apply your reason and judgement to every word and deed.

Be familiar with people, but not so intimate as to descend to vulgarity.

Base your friendship on deep emotion rather than surface whim or fancy.

Avoid entering into a quarrel but when forced into one let others beware of you.

Listen attentively to one and all but speak only to the deserving few.

You may lead a rich and comfortable life, but not indulge in a vulgar display of wealth. For exhibitionism proclaims one's character.

Do not be a borrower or lender. Borrowing dullens your management of affairs. Lending ends in loss of loan and friend.

This above all —

Be guided by the voice of your own conscience and conviction in thought, word and deed. Never falter in this discipline. Your life then will be truthful and fruitful.

MARK ANTONY'S ORATION IN *JULIUS CAESAR*

Brutus: Good countrymen, let me depart alone,
And, for my sake, stay here with Antony.
Do grace to Caesar's corpse, and grace his speech 57
Tending to Caesar's glories which Mark Antony, 58
By our permission, is allowed to make.
I do entreat you, not a man depart,
Save I alone, till Antony have spoke. *Exit.*
First Citizen: Stay, ho! and let us hear Mark Antony.
Third Citizen: Let him go up into the public chair. 63
We'll hear him. Noble Antony, go up.
Antony: For Brutus' sake I am beholding to you. 65
                    [Antony goes into the pulpit.]
Fourth Citizen: What does he say of Brutus?
Third Citizen: He says for Brutus' sake
He finds himself beholding to us all.
Fourth Citizen: 'Twere best he speak no harm of
    Brutus here!
First Citizen: This Caesar was a tyrant.
Third Citizen: Nay, that's certain.
We are blest that Rome is rid of him.
Second Citizen: Peace! Let us hear what Antony
    can say.
Antony: You gentle Romans —
Citizens: Peace, ho! Let us hear him.
Antony: Friends, Romans, countrymen, lend me
    your ears;
I come to bury Caesar, not to praise him.
The evil that men do lives after them;
The good is oft interrèd with their bones.
So let it be with Caesar. The noble Brutus
Hath told you Caesar was ambitious.
If it were so, it was a grievous fault,
And grievously hath Caesar answered it. 80
Here under leave of Brutus and the rest

For Brutus is an honourable man;
So are they all, all honourable men,
Come I to speak in Caesar's funeral.
He was my friend, faithful and just to me;   85
But Brutus says he was ambitious,
And Brutus is an honourable man.
He hath brought many captives home to Rome,
Whose ransoms did the general coffers fill.   89
Did this in Caesar seem ambitious?
When that the poor have cried, Caesar hath wept;
Ambition should be made of sterner stuff.
Yet Brutus says he was ambitious;
And Brutus is an honourable man.
You all did see that on the Lupercal
I thrice presented him a kingly crown,
Which he did thrice refuse. Was this ambition?
Yet Brutus says he was ambitious;
And sure he is an honourable man.
I speak not to disprove what Brutus spoke,   100
But here I am to speak what I do know.
You all did love him once, not without cause.
What cause withholds you then to mourn for him?
O judgement, thou art fled to brutish beasts,
And men have lost their reason! Bear with me.
My heart is in the coffin there with Caesar,
And I must pause till it come back to me.
First Citizen: Methinks there is much reason in
  his sayings.
Second Citizen: If thou consider rightly of the matter,
  Caesar has had great wrong.
Third Citizen: Has he, masters?
I fear there will a worse come in his place.
Fourth Citizen: Marked ye his words?
He would not take the crown;
Therefore 'tis certain he was not ambitious.
First Citizen: If it be found so, some will dear
  abide it.   114
Second Citizen: Poor soul! his eyes are red as fire
  with weeping.

Third Citizen: There's not a nobler man in Rome
than Antony.
Fourth Citizen: Now mark him. He begins again to
   speak.
Antony: But yesterday the word of Caesar might
Have stood against the world. Now lies he there,
And none so poor to do him reverence.   120
O masters! If I were disposed to stir
Your hearts and minds to mutiny and rage,   122
I should do Brutus wrong, and Cassius wrong,
Who, you all know, are honourable men.
I will not do them wrong. I rather choose
To wrong the dead, to wrong myself and you,
Than I will wrong such honourable men.
But here's a parchment with the seal of Caesar.
I found it in his closet; 'tis his will.   129
Let but the commons hear this testament,   130
Which, pardon me, I do not mean to read,
And they would go and kiss dead Caesar's wounds
And dip their napkins in his sacred blood;   133
Yea, beg a hair of him for memory,
And dying, mention it within their wills,
Bequeathing it as a rich legacy
Unto their issue.
Fourth Citizen: We'll hear the will! Read it, Mark
   Antony.
Citizens: The will, the will! We will hear Caesar's
   will!
Antony: Have patience, gentle friends; I must not
   read it.
It is not meet you know how Caesar loved you.   141
   You are not wood, you are not stones, but men;
And being men, hearing the will of Caesar,
It will inflame you, it will make you mad.
'Tis good you know not that you are his heirs;
For if you should, O, what would come of it?
Fourth Citizen: Read the will! We'll hear it, Antony!
You shall read us the will, Caesar's will!

Antony: Will you be patient? Will you stay
   awhile? 149
I have o'ershot myself to tell you of it. 150
I fear I wrong the honourable men
Whose daggers have stabbed Caesar; I do fear it.
Fourth Citizen: They were traitors. Honourable men!
Citizens: The will! the testament!
Second Citizen: They were villians,
Murderers! The will! Read the will!
Antony: You will compel me then to read the will?
Then make a ring about the corpse of Caesar
And let me show you him that made the will.
Shall I descend? and will you give me leave?
Citizens: Come down.
Second Citizen: Descend.
Third Citizen: You shall have leave.

                     [Antony comes down.]
Fourth Citizen: A ring! Stand round.
First Citizen: Stand from the hearse! Stand
   from the body! 165
Second Citizen: Room for Antony, most noble Antony!
Antony: Nay, press not so upon me. Stand far off. 167
Citizens: Stand back! Room! Bear back! 168
Antony: If you have tears, prepare to shed them now.
You all do know this mantle. I remember 170
The first time ever Caesar put it on.
'Twas on a summer's evening in his tent,
That day he overcame the Nervii. 173
Look, in this place ran Cassius' dagger through.
See what a rent the envious Casca made. 175
Through this the well-belovèd Brutus stabbed;
And as he plucked his cursèd steel away,
Mark how the blood of Caesar followed it,
As rushing out of doors to be resolved 179
If Brutus so unkindly knocked or no; 180
For Brutus, as you know, was Caesar's angel. 181
Judge, O you gods, how dearly Caesar loved him!
This was the most unkindest cut of all; 183

For when the noble Caesar saw him stab,
Ingratitude, more strong than traitors' arms,
Quite vanquished him. Then burst his mighty heart;
And in his mantle muffling up his face,
Even at the base of Pompey's statue   188
Which all the while ran blood, great Caesar fell.
O, what a fall was there, my countrymen!
Then I, and you, and all of us fell down,
Whilst bloody treason flourished over us.   192
O, now you weep, and I perceive you feel
The dint of pity. These are gracious drops.   194
Kind souls, what weep you when you but
   behold   195
Our Caesar's vesture wounded? Look you here!   196
Here is himself, marred as you see with traitors.   197
First Citizen: O piteous spectacle!
Second Citizen: O noble Caesar!
Third Citizen: O woeful day!
Fourth Citizen: O traitors, villians!
First Citizen: O most bloody sight!
Second Citizen: We will be revenged.
Citizens: Revenge! About! Seek! Burn!   204
Fire! Kill! Slay!
Let not a traitor live!
Antony: Stay, countrymen.   206
First Citizen: Peace there! Hear the noble Antony.
Second Citizen: We'll hear him, we'll follow him,
   we'll die with him!
Antony: Good friends, sweet friends, let me not stir
   you up
To such a sudden flood of mutiny.
They that have done this deed are honourable.
What private griefs they have, alas, I know not,   213
That made them do it. They are wise and
   honourable.
And will no doubt with reasons answer you.
I come not, friends, to steal away your hearts.
I am no orator, as Brutus is,

But, as you know me all, a plain blunt man
That love my friend; and that they know full well
That gave me public leave to speak of him.   220
For I have neither writ, nor words, nor worth,   221
Action, nor utterance, nor the power of speech   222
To stir men's blood. I only speak right on.   223
I tell you that which you yourselves do know,
Show you sweet Caesar's wounds, poor poor
   dumb mouths,
And bid them speak for me. But were I Brutus,
And Brutus Antony, there were an Antony
Would ruffle up your spirits, and put a tongue   228
In every wound of Caesar that should move
The stones of Rome to rise and mutiny.
Citizens: We'll mutiny.
First Citizen: We'll burn the house of Brutus.
Third Citizen: Away then! Come, seek the
   conspirators.
Antony: Yet hear me, countrymen. Yet hear me speak.
Citizens: Peace, ho! Hear Antony, most noble
   Antony!
Antony: Why, friends, you go to do you know
   not what.
Wherein hath Caesar thus deserved your loves?
Alas, you know not! I must tell you then.
You have forgot the will I told you of.
Citizens: Most true! The will! Let's stay and hear
   the will.
Antony: Here is the will, and under Caesar's seal.
To every Roman citizen he gives,
To every several man, seventy-five drachmas.   242
Second Citizen: Most noble Caesar! We'll revenge
   his death!
Third Citizen: O royal Caesar!   244
Antony: Hear me with patience.
Citizens: Peace, ho!
Antony: Moreover, he hath left you all his walks, 247
His private arbours, and new-planted orchards,   248

On this side Tiber; he hath left them you,
And to your heirs for ever — common pleasures, 250
To walk abroad and recreate yourselves.
Here was a Caesar! When comes such another?
First Citizen: Never, never! Come, away, away!
We'll burn his body in the holy place 254
And with the brands fire the traitors' houses.
Take up the body.
Second Citizen: Go fetch fire!
Third Citizen: Pluck down benches! 258
Fourth Citizen: Pluck down forms, windows,
   anything! 259
                    Exit Citizens [with the body].
Antony: Now let it work. Mischief, thou art afoot, 260
Take thou what course thou wilt.

           — from *Julius Caesar* by William Shakespeare
                    Act III, Scene II, Lines 55 - 261

Glossary

Line

Line	Word		Meaning
60	entreat	:	request
65	beholding	:	obliged to address you
76	interrèd	:	buried (into earth)
81	under leave	:	with permission
89	ransoms	:	payment for freeing captives
95	Lupercal	:	a Roman festival
114	abide it	:	dearly pay for it
122	mutiny	:	revolt
128	parchment	:	document
129	closet	:	chamber
130	commons	:	public
	testament	:	will

136 bequeathing	:	leaving by will to others
legacy	:	rich inheritance
137 issue	:	children
141 meet	:	proper, fitting
150 o'ershot myself	:	transgressed
165 hearse	:	coffin
170 mantle	:	a cloak
173 Nervii	:	place where Caesar won a famous battle
175 rent	:	portion torn by dagger
177 cursèd steel	:	an example of Dramatic Irony
179 - 181	:	the very blood rushing out of Caesar's wounds seems to enquire if Brutus, so fondly loved by Caesar, could have done such a dastardly act
resolved	:	settled, decided, solved
angel	:	an attendant or guardian
183 This was the most	:	a very well-known construction
unkindest cut of all		using a double superlative, which is grammatically incorrect but used here to indicate the inexplicable dastardliness of the act.
187 muffling	:	covering
192 treason	:	treachery
194 dint of pity	:	mark of pity
213 private griefs	:	thwarted selfish ambitions
220 public leave	:	permission to speak in public
225 poor poor dumb mouths	:	an example of epic repetition. Used for heightening emphasis.

226 - 227 but were I Brutus, and Brutus Antony	:	if I was Brutus, and Brutus was Antony
228 ruffle up	:	arouse, agitate
242 every several man	:	to each and every man
drachmas	:	currency of that era
248 arbours	:	shaded walks
249 Tiber	:	river on which Rome stands
251 walk abroad	:	walk in the open
255 brands		burning torches
fire	:	burn down

Julius Caesar was a Roman emperor. A noble soul. Brutus with other conspirators assassinated Caesar. He convinced the masses that Caesar was a selfish tyrant, detrimental to the state. The people accepted Brutus' dastardly action as an honourable service to the nation.

Mark Antony was a true friend of Caesar's. He learnt too late of the conspirators' diabolical plan and Caesar's assassination. He decided to expose their treachery and managed to obtain Brutus' permission to speak at Caesar's funeral. Brutus, having permitted Antony to speak, left the scene of the funeral.

Antony faced an emotionally charged mob. They were led to believe that Brutus was honourable and the assassination justified. Antony now had the tremendous task of turning the whole mob against Brutus. He went about it cautiously, brilliantly to expose the conspirators.

The oration of Antony is an outstanding piece of English literature. Antony worked on the psychology of the mob. Turned their mind around from their state of infatuated admiration to infuriated rage against Brutus and the rest.

Antony handled the whole situation with perfect objectivity. He felt it his obligatory duty to expose the villainy of the conspirators. Went about it meticulously in a spirit of detachment. At the end of his brilliant oration he left the result for destiny to work itself out —

> *Mischief, thou art afoot,*
> *Take thou what course thou wilt.*

LETTER TO
THE EARL OF CHESTERFIELD

"TO THE RIGHT HONOURABLE
THE EARL OF CHESTERFIELD."

February 7, 1755.

"MY LORD,

"I have been lately informed, by the proprietor of the World, that two papers, in which my Dictionary is recommended to the publick, were written by your Lordship. To be so distinguished, is an honour, which, being very little accustomed to favours from the great, I know not well how to receive, or in what terms to acknowledge.

"When, upon some slight encouragement, I first visited your Lordship, I was overpowered, like the rest of mankind, by the enchantment of your address, and could not forbear to wish that I might boast myself *Le vainqueur du vainqueur de la terre;* — that I might obtain that regard for which I saw the world contending; but I found my attendance so little encouraged, that neither pride nor modesty would suffer me to continue it. When I had once addressed your Lordship in publick, I had exhausted all the art of pleasing which a retired and uncourtly scholar can possess. I had done all that I could; and no man is well pleased to have his all neglected, be it ever so little.

"Seven years, my Lord, have now past, since I waited in your outward rooms, or was repulsed from your door; during which time I have been pushing on my work through difficulties, of which it is useless to complain, and have brought it, at last, to the verge of publication, without one act of assistance, one word of encouragement, or one smile of favour. Such treatment I did not expect, for I never had a Patron before.

"The shepherd in Virgil grew at last acquainted with Love, and found him a native of the rocks.

"Is not a Patron, my Lord, one who looks with unconcern on a man struggling for life in the water, and, when he has reached ground, encumbers him with help? The notice which you have been pleased to take of my labours, had it been early, had been kind; but it has been delayed till I am indifferent, and cannot enjoy it; till I am solitary, and cannot impart it; till I am known, and do not want it. I hope it is no very cynical asperity, not to confess obligations where no benefit has been received, or to be unwilling that the Publick should consider me as owing that to a Patron, which Providence has enabled me to do for myself.

"Having carried on my work thus far with so little obligation to any favourer of learning, I shall not be disappointed though I should conclude it, if less be possible, with less; for I have been long wakened from that dream of hope, in which I once boasted myself with so much exultation,

"My Lord,
"Your Lordship's most humble
"Most obedient servant,
"SAM. JOHNSON."

Glossary

lately	:	recently
The World	:	name of newspaper
publick	:	public

forbear	:	check myself
le vainqueur du vainqueur de la terre	:	the conqueror of the conqueror of the world
contending	:	striving for
suffer	:	permit
waited in your outward rooms, or was repulsed from your door	:	I was neither asked to wait nor asked to leave
Virgil	:	Roman poet (70 - 19 B.C.)
encumbers him with help	:	overwhelming with unwanted, unnecessary help
solitary	:	alone. Johnson's wife had died meanwhile, in 1752
impart	:	share
cynical	:	pessimistic, complaining, grumbling
asperity	:	harshness, rudeness
if less be possible, with less	:	acknowledgement of the grace of Providence above all patronage in human achievements

Samuel Johnson was a literary genius. He published the first English dictionary. While preparing the dictionary he was introduced to the Earl of Chesterfied to patronise its publication. The Earl offered to help but for seven years did nothing to support Johnson. However, Johnson managed to publish the dictionary on his own. Having heard of its publication Chesterfield rushed articles to the newspaper 'The World' recommending the dictionary to the public. Johnson was humiliated by the lord's indifference and vanity. It was then that he wrote this famous letter. A valuable contribution to English literature.

LAODAMIA

"With sacrifice before the rising morn
Vows have I made by fruitless hope inspired;
And from the infernal Gods, 'mid shades forlorn
Of night, my slaughtered Lord have I required:
Celestial pity I again implore; —
Restore him to my sight — great Jove, restore!"   6

So speaking, and by fervent love endowed
With faith, the Suppliant heavenward lifts her
   hands;
While, like the sun emerging from a cloud,
Her countenance brightens — and her eye
   expands;
Her bosom heaves and spreads, her stature grows;
And she expects the issue in repose.   12

O terror! what hath she perceived? — O joy!
What doth she look on? — whom doth she
   behold?
Her Hero slain upon the beach of Troy?
His vital presence? his corporeal mould?
It is — if sense deceive her not — 'tis He!
And a God leads him, wingèd Mercury!   18

Mild Hermes spake — and touched her with his
   wand
That calms all fear; "Such grace hath crowned thy
   prayer,
Laodamía! that at Jove's command
Thy Husband walks the paths of upper air:
He comes to tarry with thee three hours' space;
Accept the gift, behold him face to face!"   24

Forth sprang the impassioned Queen her Lord to
   clasp;
Again that consummation she essayed;
But unsubstantial Form eludes her grasp
As often as that eager grasp was made.
The Phantom parts — but parts to re-unite,
And re-assume his place before her sight.   30

"Protesiláus, lo! thy guide is gone!
Confirm, I pray, the vision with thy voice:
This is our palace, — yonder is thy throne;
Speak, and the floor thou tread'st on will rejoice.
Not to appal me have the gods bestowed
This precious boon; and blest a sad abode."   36

"Great Jove, Laodamia! doth not leave
His gifts imperfect:— Spectre though I be,
I am not sent to scare thee or deceive;
But in reward of thy fidelity.
And something also did my worth obtain;
For fearless virtue bringeth boundless gain.   42

"Thou knowest, the Delphic oracle foretold
That the first Greek who touched the Trojan strand
Should die; but me the threat could not withold:
A generous cause a victim did demand;
And forth I leapt upon the sandy plain;
A self-devoted chief — by Hector slain."   48

"Supreme of Heroes — bravest, noblest, best!
Thy matchless courage I bewail no more,
Which then, when tens of thousands were deprest
By doubt, propelled thee to the fatal shore;
Thou found'st — and I forgive thee — here thou
   art —
A nobler counsellor than my poor heart.   54

"But thou, though capable of sternest deed,
Wert kind as resolute, and good as brave;
And he, whose power restores thee, hath decreed
Thou should'st elude the malice of the grave:
Redundant are thy locks, thy lips as fair
As when their breath enriched Thessalian air.   60

"No Spectre greets me, — no vain Shadow this;
Come, blooming Hero, place thee by my side!
Give, on this well-known couch, one nuptial kiss
To me, this day, a second time thy bride!"
Jove frowned in heaven: the conscious Parcæ threw
Upon those roseate lips a Stygian hue.   66

"This visage tells thee that my doom is past:
Nor should the change be mourned, even if the joys
Of sense were able to return as fast
And surely as they vanish. Earth destroys
Those raptures duly — Erebus disdains:
Calm pleasures there abide — majestic pains.   72

"Be taught, O faithful Consort, to control
Rebellious passion: for the Gods approve
The depth, and not the tumult, of the soul;
A fervent, not ungovernable, love.
Thy transports moderate; and meekly mourn
When I depart, for brief is my sojourn —"   78

"Ah wherefore? — Did not Hercules by force
Wrest from the guardian Monster of the tomb
Alcestis, a reanimated corse,
Given back to dwell on earth in vernal bloom?
Medea's spells dispersed the weight of years,
And Æson stood a youth 'mid youthful peers.   84

"The Gods to us are merciful — and they
Yet further may relent: for mightier far
Than strength of nerve and sinew, or the sway
Of magic potent over sun and star,
Is love, though oft to agony distrest,
And though his favourite seat be feeble
   woman's breast.   90

"But if thou goest, I follow —" "Peace!" he said, —
She looked upon him and was calmed and cheered;
The ghastly colour from his lips had fled;
In his deportment, shape, and mien, appeared
Elysian beauty, melancholy grace,
Brought from a pensive though a happy place.   96

He spake of love, such love as Spirits feel
In worlds whose course is equable and pure;
No fears to beat away — no strife to heal —
The past unsighed for, and the future sure;
Spake of heroic arts in graver mood
Revived, with finer harmony pursued;   102

Of all that is most beauteous — imaged there
In happier beauty; more pellucid streams,
An ampler ether, a diviner air,
And fields invested with purpureal gleams;
Climes which the sun, who sheds the brightest day
Earth knows, is all unworthy to survey.   108

Yet there the Soul shall enter which hath earned
That privilege by virtue. — "Ill," said he,
"The end of man's existence I discerned,
Who from ignoble games and revelry
Could draw, when we had parted, vain delight,
While tears were thy best pastime, day and night; 114

"And while my youthful peers before my eyes
(Each hero following his peculiar bent)
Prepared themselves for glorious enterprise
By martial sports, — or, seated in the tent,
Chieftains and kings in council were detained;
What time the fleet at Aulis lay enchained.   120

"The wished-for wind was given: — I then revolved
The oracle, upon the silent sea;
And, if no worthier led the way, resolved
That, of a thousand vessels, mine should be
The foremost prow in pressing to the strand, —
Mine the first blood that tinged the Trojan sand.   126

"Yet bitter, oft-times bitter, was the pang
When of thy loss I thought, belovèd Wife!
On thee too fondly did my memory hang,
And on the joys we shared in mortal life, —
The paths which we had trod — these fountains,
    flowers;
My new-planned cities, and unfinished towers.   132

"But should suspense permit the Foe to cry,
'Behold they tremble! — haughty their array,
Yet of their number no one dares to die?'
In soul I swept the indignity away:
Old frailties then recurred:— but lofty thought,
In act embodied, my deliverance wrought.   138

"And Thou, though strong in love, art all too weak
In reason, in self-government too slow;
I counsel thee by fortitude to seek
Our blest re-union in the shades below.
The invisible world with thee hath sympathized;
Be thy affections raised and solemnised.   144

"Learn, by a mortal yearning, to ascend —
Seeking a higher object. Love was given,
Encouraged, sanctioned, chiefly for that end;
For this the passion to excess was driven —
That self might be annulled: her bondage prove
The fetters of a dream opposed to love." —   150

Aloud she shrieked! for Hermes reappears!
Round the dear Shade she would have clung —
   'tis vain:
The hours are past — too brief had they been
   years;
And him no mortal effort can detain:
Swift, toward the realms that know not earthly
   day,
He through the portal takes his silent way,
And on the palace-floor a lifeless corse She lay.   156

Thus, all in vain exhorted and reproved,
She perished; and, as for a wilful crime,
By the just Gods whom no weak pity moved,
Was doomed to wear out her appointed time,
Apart from happy Ghosts, that gather flowers
Of blissful quiet 'mid unfading bowers.   162

— Yet tears to human suffering are due;
And mortal hopes defeated and o'erthrown
Are mourned by man, and not by man alone,
As fondly he believes. — Upon the side
Of Hellespont (such faith was entertained)
A knot of spiry trees for ages grew
From out the tomb of him for whom she died;
And ever, when such stature they had gained
That Illium's walls were subject to their view,
The trees' tall summits withered at the sight;
A constant interchange of growth and blight!   173

— William Wordsworth

70

Glossary

Line

6	Jove	:	Chief of Roman gods
12	issue in repose	:	emergence of Laodamia's husband in response to her consistent prayer
16	corporeal mould	:	bodily presence
19	Hermes	:	the Roman god, Mercury
23	tarry	:	stay
29	Phantom	:	apparition, spirit
31	Protesiláus	:	Laodamia's husband, a heroic warrior
35	appal	:	terrify
38	spectre	:	apparition, spirit
43	Delphic oracle	:	prophecy given at the Delphic temple that the first Greek soldier to set foot on Trojan soil would be killed
48	Hector	:	heroic Trojan prince, son of king Priam of Troy
65	Parcæ	:	Roman goddess of colour
66	Stygian hue	:	black colour
71	Erebus	:	dark, gloomy cavernous hell
72	there	:	refers to heaven
79 - 84		:	Greek mythological episodes wherein beings returned to life, regained youth
79	Hercules	:	a Greek hero, famed for his superhuman strength
81	Alcestis	:	in Greek mythology, the wife of Admetus. He was doomed to die, she saved him by offering to die in his place. Hercules wrestled

			with the messenger of death, brought her back to life
83	Medea	:	a witch in Greek mythology
86	relent	:	relax severity
94	deportment	:	bearing
	mien	:	facial expression
95	Elysian	:	heavenly
	melancholy grace	:	pleasing sadness
103	beauteous	:	beautiful
104	pellucid	:	transparent, clear
106	purpureal gleams	:	purple sheens
137	frailties	:	emotional infirrnity
141	fortitude	:	strength in adversity
149	bondage	:	attachment
157	exhorted	:	advised
	reproved	:	rebuked
162	bowers	:	shady retreat with trees and plants
164	mortal hopes	:	desires
173	blight	:	withering

Protesiláus was a Greek prince. The hero of a Greek armada that sailed to Troy. An oracle had prophesied that the first Greek soldier landing on Trojan soil would be killed. As the armada was approaching Troy the Greeks were debating who should land first. Meanwhile, Protesiláus jumped ashore. He was killed.

Protesiláus' wife, Laodamia was very much upset. She perceived her husband's death as a great injustice meted out to her. She pleaded to Jove, the supreme

God, to restore her husband to her. Jove responded to her prayer. But granted her just three hours of Protesiláus' company.

The poem starts with Protesiláus' return to earth escorted by god Mercury. It contains the conversation between Laodamia and Protesiláus in those three hours. The highlight of the poem is the brilliant philosophy that Protesiláus addresses to Laodamia.

The poem depicts woman's infatuation for man. Laodamia's terrible attachment to her husband Protesiláus. Like any other attachment, her infatuation led to her own ruination. The poet points out that attachment culminates in total loss and destruction.

ANDREA DEL SARTO

But do not let us quarrel any more,
No, my Lucrezia; bear with me for once:
Sit down and all shall happen as you wish.
You turn your face, but does it bring your heart?
I'll work then for your friend's friend, never fear,   5
Treat his own subject after his own way,
Fix his own time, accept too his own price,
And shut the money into this small hand
When next it takes mine. Will it? tenderly?
Oh, I'll content him, — but tomorrow, Love!   10
I often am much wearier than you think,
This evening more than usual, and it seems
As if — forgive now — should you let me sit
Here by the window with your hand in mine
And look a half-hour forth on Fiesole,   15
Both of one mind, as married people use,
Quietly, quietly the evening through,
I might get up tomorrow to my work
Cheerful and fresh as ever. Let us try.
Tomorrow, how you shall be glad for this!   20
Your soft hand is a woman of itself,
And mine the man's bared breast she curls inside.
Don't count the time lost, neither; you must serve
For each of the five pictures we require:
It saves a model. So! keep looking so —   25
My serpentining beauty, rounds on rounds!
— How could you ever prick those perfect ears,
Even to put the pearl there! oh, so sweet —
My face, my moon, my everybody's moon,
Which everybody looks on and calls his,   30
And, I suppose, is looked on by in turn,
While she looks — no one's: very dear, no less.
You smile? why, there's my picture ready made,
There's what we painters call our harmony!

A common greyness silvers everything, —   35
All in a twilight, you and I alike
— You, at the point of your first pride in me
(That's gone you know), — but I, at every point;
My youth, my hope, my art, being all toned down
To yonder sober pleasant Fiesole.   40
There's the bell clinking from the chapel-top;
That length of convent-wall across the way
Holds the trees safer, huddled more inside;
The last monk leaves the garden; days decrease,
And autumn grows, autumn in everything.   45
Eh? the whole seems to fall into a shape
As if I saw alike my work and self
And all that I was born to be and do,
A twilight-piece. Love, we are in God's hand.
How strange now, looks the life He makes us
   lead;   50
So free we seem, so fettered fast we are!
I feel He laid the fetter: let it lie!
This chamber for example — turn your head —
All that's behind us! You don't understand
Nor care to understand about my art,   55
But you can hear at least when people speak:
And that cartoon, the second from the door —
It is the thing, Love! so such things should be —
Behold Madonna! — I am bold to say.
I can do with my pencil what I know,   60
What I see, what at bottom of my heart
I wish for, if I ever wish so deep —
Do easily, too — when I say, perfectly,
I do not boast, perhaps: yourself are judge,
Who listened to the Legate's talk last week,   65
And just as much they used to say in France.
At any rate 'tis easy, all of it!
No sketches first, no studies, that's long past:
I do what many dream of, all their lives,
— Dream? strive to do, and agonise to do,   70
And fail in doing. I could count twenty such

On twice your fingers, and not leave this town,
Who strive — you don't know how the others strive
To paint a little thing like that you smeared
Carelessly passing with your robes afloat, —   75
Yet do much less, so much less, Someone says,
(I know his name, no matter) — so much less!
Well, less is more, Lucrezia: I am judged.
There burns a truer light of God in them,
In their vexed beating stuffed and stopped-up
    brain,   80
Heart, or whate'er else, than goes on to prompt
This low-pulsed forthright craftsman's hand of
    mine.
Their works drop groundward, but themselves,
    I know,
Reach many a time a heaven that's shut to me,
Enter and take their place there sure enough,   85
Though they come back and cannot tell the world.
My works are nearer heaven, but I sit here.
The sudden blood of these men! at a word —
Praise them, it boils, or blame them, it boils too.
I, painting from myself and to myself,   90
Know what I do, am unmoved by men's blame
Or their praise either. Somebody remarks
Morello's outline there is wrongly traced,
His hue mistaken; what of that? or else,
Rightly traced and well ordered; what of that?   95
Speak as they please, what does the mountain care?
Ah, but a man's reach should exceed his grasp,
Or what's a Heaven for? All is silver-grey
Placid and perfect with my art: the worse!
I know both what I want and what might gain,   100
And yet how profitless to know, to sigh
'Had I been two, another and myself,
Our head would have o'erlooked the world!' No
    doubt.
Yonder's a work now, of that famous youth
The Urbinate who died five years ago.   105

('Tis copied, George Vasari sent it me.)
Well, I can fancy how he did it all,
Pouring his soul, with kings and popes to see,
Reaching, that Heaven might so replenish him,
Above and through his art — for it gives way;   110
That arm is wrongly put — and there again —
A fault to pardon in the drawing's lines,
Its body, so to speak: its soul is right,
He means right — that, a child may understand.
Still, what an arm! and I could alter it: 115
But all the play, the insight and the stretch —
Out of me, out of me! And wherefore out?
Had you enjoined them on me, given me soul,
We might have risen to Rafael, I and you!
Nay, Love, you did give all I asked, I think —   120
More than I merit, yes, by many times.
But had you — oh, with the same perfect brow,
And perfect eyes, and more than perfect mouth,
And the low voice my soul hears, as a bird
The fowler's pipe, and follows to the snare —   125
Had you, with these the same, but brought a mind!
Some women do so. Had the mouth there urged
'God and the glory! never care for gain.
The present by the future, what is that?
Live for fame, side by side with Agnolo!   130
Rafael is waiting: Up to God, all three!'
I might have done it for you. So it seems:
Perhaps not. All is as God over-rules.
Beside, incentives come from the soul's self;
The rest avail not. Why do I need you?   135
What wife had Rafael, or has Agnolo?
In this world, who can do a thing, will not;
And who would do it, cannot, I perceive:
Yet the will's somewhat — somewhat, too, the
    power —
And thus we half-men struggle. At the end,   140
God, I conclude, compensates, punishes.
'Tis safer for me, if the award be strict,

That I am something underrated here,
Poor this long while, despised, to speak the truth.
I dared not, do you know, leave home all day,   145
For fear of chancing on the Paris lords.
The best is when they pass and look aside;
But they speak sometimes; I must bear it all.
Well may they speak! That Francis, that first time,
And that long festal year at Fontainebleau!   150
I surely then could sometimes leave the ground,
Put on the glory, Rafael's daily wear,
In that humane great monarch's golden look, —
One finger in his beard or twisted curl
Over his mouth's good mark that made the
      smile,   155
One arm about my shoulder, round my neck,
The jingle of his gold chain in my ear,
I painting proudly with his breath on me,
All his court round him, seeing with his eyes,
Such frank French eyes, and such a fire of souls   160
Profuse, my hand kept plying by those hearts, —
And, best of all, this, this, this face beyond,
This in the background, waiting on my work,
To crown the issue with a last reward!
A good time, was it not, my kingly days?   165
And had you not grown restless ... but I know —
'Tis done and past; 'twas right, my instinct said;
Too live the life grew, golden and not grey,
And I'm the weak-eyed bat no sun should tempt
Out of the grange whose four walls make his
      world.   170
How could it end in any other way?
You called me, and I came home to your heart.
The triumph was — to reach and stay there; since
I reached it ere the triumph, what is lost?
Let my hands frame your face in your hair's
      gold,   175
You beautiful Lucrezia that are mine!
'Rafael did this, Andrea painted that;

The Roman's is the better when you pray,
But still the other's Virgin was his wife —'
Men will excuse me. I am glad to judge   180
Both pictures in your presence; clearer grows
My better fortune, I resolve to think.
For, do you know, Lucrezia, as God lives,
Said one day Agnolo, his very self,
To Rafael ... I have known it all these years...   185
(When the young man was flaming out his thoughts
Upon a palace-wall for Rome to see,
Too lifted up in heart because of it)
'Friend, there's a certain sorry little scrub
Goes up and down our Florence, none cares how,   190
Who, were he set to plan and execute
As you are, pricked on by your popes and kings,
Would bring the sweat into that brow of yours!'
To Rafael's! — And indeed the arm is wrong.
I hardly dare ... yet, only you to see,   195
Give the chalk here — quick, thus the line should go!
Ay, but the soul! he's Rafael! rub it out!
Still, all I care for, if he spoke the truth,
(What he? why, who but Michael Agnolo?
Do you forget already words like those?)   200
If really there was such a chance, so lost, —
Is, whether you're — not grateful — but more pleased.
Well, let me think so. And you smile indeed!
This hour has been an hour! Another smile?
If you would sit thus by me every night   205
I should work better, do you comprehend?
I mean that I should earn more, give you more.
See, it is settled dusk now; there's a star;
Morello's gone, the watch-lights show the wall,
The cue-owls speak the name we call them by.   210
Come from the window, love, — come in, at last,

Inside the melancholy little house
We built to be so gay with. God is just.
King Francis may forgive me: oft at nights
When I look up from painting, eyes tired out,   215
The walls become illumined, brick from brick
Distinct, instead of mortar, fierce bright gold,
That gold of his I did cement them with!
Let us but love each other. Must you go?
That Cousin here again? he waits outside?   220
Must see you — you, and not with me? Those
  loans?
More gaming debts to pay? you smiled for that?
Well, let smiles buy me! have you more to spend?
While hand and eye and something of a heart
Are left me, work's my ware, and what's it
  worth?   225
I'll pay my fancy. Only let me sit
The grey remainder of the evening out,
Idle, you call it, and muse perfectly
How I could paint, were I but back in France,
One picture, just one more — the Virgin's face,   230
Not your's this time! I want you at my side
To hear them — that is, Michael Agnolo —
Judge all I do and tell you of its worth.
Will you? Tomorrow, satisfy your friend.
I take the subjects for his corridor,   235
Finish the portrait out of hand — there, there,
And throw him in another thing or two
If he demurs; the whole should prove enough
To pay for this same Cousin's freak. Beside,
What's better and what's all I care about,   240
Get you the thirteen scudi for the ruff!
Love, does that please you? Ah, but what does he,
The Cousin! what does he to please you more?

  I am grown peaceful as old age tonight.
I regret little, I would change still less.   245
Since there my past life lies, why alter it?
The very wrong to Francis! — it is true

I took his coin, was tempted and complied,
And built this house and sinned, and all is said.
My father and my mother died of want.   250
Well, had I riches of my own? you see
How one gets rich! Let each one bear his lot.
They were born poor, lived poor, and poor they
    died:
And I have laboured somewhat in my time
And not been paid profusely. Some good son   255
Paint my two hundred pictures — let him try!
No doubt, there's something strikes a balance. Yes,
You loved me quite enough, it seems tonight.
This must suffice me here. What would one have?
In heaven, perhaps, new chances, one more
    chance —   260
Four great walls in the New Jerusalem,
Meted on each side by the angel's reed,
For Leonard, Rafael, Agnolo and me
To cover — the three first without a wife,
While I have mine! So — still they overcome   265
Because there's still Lucrezia, — as I choose.

Again the Cousin's whistle! Go, my Love.

— Robert Browning

Glossary

Line

2	bear with me	:	tolerate me
4	you turn your face	:	you face me
5	friend's friend	:	refers to Lucrezia's lover's friend
10	but tomorrow	:	Andrea promises he will paint for her lover tomorrow
15	Fiesole	:	suburb of Florence
21	a woman of itself	:	softness itself

22	and mine the man's bared breast	:	and my hand hard as man's chest
26	serpentining	:	curving
29	my face, my moon, my everybody's moon	:	your face (belonging to me) is as beautiful and comforting as the moon
34	harmony	:	artistically agreeable
35	a common greyness silvers	:	her original pride in him has waned but for a condescending smile
38-48		:	compares his life to autumn marking the end of his glory
39	toned down	:	mellowed
40	sober	:	dull
41	clinking	:	ringing
43	safer	:	more confined
45	autumn in everything	:	entire atmosphere of autumn
49	twilight-piece	:	gloomy, referring to his life and work
49-53		:	speaks of Andrea's resignation to his life of extreme freedom and bondage
53	turn your head	:⎫	
54	all that's behind us	:⎭	look at all my works of art
57	cartoon	:	a drawing on paper as design for painting
59	Madonna	:	Virgin Mary
65	Legate's talk	:	the praise that the Legate, a church dignitary, bestowed on his work
69	many	:	refers to great artists
78	less is more, Lucrezia: I am judged	:	though inferior in quality to Andrea others gain wealth and praise from society
79-82		:	the other artists with limited

			talent were inspired, whereas Andrea's superior talent lacked lustre due to his infatuation for his wife
79	truer light of God	:	(divine) inspiration
82	low-pulsed	:	lacking inspiration
	forthright	:	talented
83	drop groundward	:	lack Andrea's perfection
88	sudden blood	:	impulsiveness
88-89	at a word ... too	:	affected by praise and censure
90	from myself and to myself	:	for my own satisfaction
93	Morello's outline	:	painting of mountain, Morello
96	what does the mountain care	:	like a mountain a true artist is indifferent to fame or blame
97	reach	:	aim, ideal
99	the worse	:	a talent wasted
102	had I been two	:	two distinct individuals — one for painting, the other for Lucrezia
105	Urbinate	:	born in Urbino, referring to Rafael
106	George Vasari	:	a famous Italian painter
109	reaching, that Heaven might so replenish him	:	name and fame may satisfy Rafael's yearning
118	given me soul	:	inspired me
125	fowler	:	bird-catcher
127	the mouth	:	your words
129	the present by the future, what is that	:	what is the purpose of acting in the present for future gain, fame
130	Agnolo	:	great Italian painter Michelangelo
134	incentives	:	inspiration
137-138		:	those talented to paint lack the

			desire, and those with the desire lack talent
146	Paris lords	:	King Francis gave Andrea money which he misappropriated. The reference here is to this Paris connection
149	Francis	:	his royal patron, King of France
150	Fontainebleau	:	a town near Paris where King Francis' palace is located
154	twisted curl	:	moustache
162	this, this, this face	:	Lucrezia's face, a backdrop to all of Andrea's works
168	too live the life grew golden and not grey	:	Andrea seeking Lucrezia's favour, tries to justify his return from France
170	grange	:	barn
174	it	:	Lucrezia's love
175 - 207		:	Andrea confesses that his satisfaction in Lucrezia's love is beyond Michelangelo's praise of Andrea's art to Rafael
178	Roman's	:	Rafael's
179	other's Virgin	:	referring to Andrea's "Madonna"
181	both pictures	:	one by Rafael, other by Andrea
186	the young man	:	Rafael
189	little scrub	:	insignificant person
192	pricked on	:	encouraged
209	Morello's	:	of mountain-peak
210	cue-owls	:	the Scops owl. Its cry is a ringing "ki-ou", hence the name
212	melancholy	:	sad
213	gay	:	happy
218	That gold of his I did cement them with	:	the money of King Francis that Andrea used to build their house

226	fancy	:	love
234	will you	:	be with me for a while
235	subjects	:	themes for the painting
236	out of hand	:	easily
238	demurs	:	complains
239	freak	:	whimsical disposition
241	scudi	:	silver coin
	ruff	:	a kind of neck-wear
255	some good son	:	brother of Andrea, good but not talented
262	meted	:	measured
	reed	:	measuring-rod
263	Leonard	:	Leonardo da Vinci
265	they overcome	:	they are overcome

Andrea del Sarto (1487-1531 A.D.) was one of the greatest painters of his time known as the faultless painter. An artist of the calibre of Leonardo da Vinci, Michelangelo or Rafael. Admitted in the Poem by Rafael himself as being superior to him.

This celebrated painter of Florence produced several outstanding works of art. He was endowed with a remarkable readiness, certainty of hand and unhesitating firmness in his painting. His painting gained for him the pre-eminent title *Andrea senxa errori* – Andrew the unerring. The youth of twenty-three was already the best fresco-painter in central Italy. Barely rivalled by Rafael, who was older by four years. Michelangelo's Sistine frescoes were then only in a preliminary stage.

Andrea fell in love with Lucrezia, wife of a hatter named Carlo Recanati. The hatter died opportunely. Andrea married Lucrezia on 26 December 1512. She was a very beautiful woman. Painted by her lover-husband as Madonna and otherwise. Even in painting other women his infatuation made them resemble Lucrezia.

Before the end of 1516, a composition of his paintings including that of Madonna were sent to the French court. The art-loving monarch, Francis, was much impressed and invited Andrea to Paris. Andrea journeyed thither and was handsomely remunerated. Lucrezia, however, wrote urging his return to Italy. The king assented with the understanding that his absence from France would be short. He was entrusted with a sum of money to be used to purchase works of art for his royal patron. Andrea, instead, spent the King's money in building a house in Florence for his wife.

In this poem Robert Browning highlights the devastating influence of a man's infatuation for woman. How it destroys a person and his achievements. Andrea del Sarto's art was acclaimed to excel that of other greats. But his infatuation took the toll of a king's patronage, his career, reputation and even his beloved Lucrezia. Since Lucrezia had her own lover and was totally indifferent towards Andrea.

A blind infatuation with a woman has reduced a great artist to nothing. Causing the loss of personality and the very object of infatuation.

SOHRAB AND RUSTUM

[The source of this poem is a translation of the
"Shah Nameh," a Persian national epic by Firdausi.]

AN EPISODE

And the first grey of morning filled the east,   1
And the fog rose out of the Oxus stream.
But all the Tartar camp along the stream
Was hushed, and still the men were plunged in
    sleep;
Sohrab alone, he slept not; all night long   5
He had lain wakeful, tossing on his bed;
But when the grey dawn stole into his tent,
He rose, and clad himself, and girt his sword,
And took his horseman's cloak, and left his tent,
And went abroad into the cold wet fog,   10
Through the dim camp to Peran-Wisa's tent.
  Through the black Tartar tents he passed, which
    stood
Clustering like bee-hives on the low flat strand
Of Oxus, where the summer-floods o'erflow
When the sun melts the snows in high Pamere;   15
Through the black tents he passed, o'er that low
    strand
And to a hillock came, a little back
From the stream's brink — the spot where first a
    boat,
Crossing the stream in summer, scrapes the land.
The men of former times had crowned the top   20
With a clay fort; but that was fallen, and now
The Tartars built there Peran-Wisa's tent,
A dome of laths, and o'er it felts were spread.
And Sohrab came there, and went in, and stood
Upon the thick piled carpets in the tent,   25

And found the old man sleeping on his bed
Of rugs and felts, and near him lay his arms.
And Peran-Wisa heard him, though the step
Was dulled; for he slept light, an old man's sleep;
And he rose quickly on one arm, and said: —   30
   'Who art thou? for it is not yet clear dawn.
Speak! is there news, or any night alarm?'
   But Sohrab came to the bedside, and said: —
'Thou know'st me, Peran-Wisa! it is I.
The sun is not yet risen, and the foe   35
Sleep; but I sleep not; all night long I lie
Tossing and wakeful, and I come to thee.
For so did King Afrasiab bid me seek
Thy counsel, and to heed thee as thy son,
In Samarcand, before the army marched;   40
And I will tell thee what my heart desires.
Thou know'st if, since from Ader-baijan first
I came among the Tartars and bore arms,
I have still served Afrasiab well, and shown,
At my boy's years, the courage of a man.   45
This too thou know'st, that while I still bear on
The conquering Tartar ensigns through the world,
And beat the Persians back on every field,
I seek one man, one man, and one alone —
Rustum, my father; who I hoped should greet,   50
Should one day greet, upon some well-fought field,
His not unworthy, not inglorious son.
So I long hoped, but him I never find.
Come then, hear now, and grant me what I ask.
Let the two armies rest to-day; but I   55
Will challenge forth the bravest Persian lords
To meet me, man to man; if I prevail,
Rustum will surely hear it; if I fall —
Old man, the dead need no one, claim no kin.
Dim is the rumour of a common fight,   60
Where host meets host, and many names are sunk;
But of a single combat fame speaks clear.'
   He spoke; and Peran-Wisa took the hand

Of the young man in his, and sighed, and said: —
  'O Sohrab, an unquiet heart is thine!   65
Canst thou not rest among the Tartar chiefs,
And share the battle's common chance with us
Who love thee, but must press for ever first,
In single fight incurring single risk,
To find a father thou hast never seen?   70
That were far best, my son, to stay with us
Unmurmuring; in our tents, while it is war,
And when 'tis truce, then in Afrasiab's towns.
But, if this one desire indeed rules all,
To seek out Rustum — seek him not through
    fight!   75
Seek him in peace, and carry to his arms,
O Sohrab, carry an unwounded son!
But far hence seek him, for he is not here.
For now it is not as when I was young,
When Rustum was in front of every fray;   80
But now he keeps apart, and sits at home,
In Seistan, with Zal, his father old.
Whether that his own mighty strength at last
Feels the abhorred approaches of old age,
Or in some quarrel with the Persian King.   85
There go! — Thou wilt not? Yet my heart forebodes
Danger or death awaits thee on this field.
Fain would I know thee safe and well, though lost
To us; fain therefore send thee hence, in peace
To seek thy father, not seek single fights   90
In vain; but who can keep the lion's cub
From ravening, and who govern Rustum's son?
Go, I will grant thee what thy heart desires.'
  So said he, and dropped Sohrab's hand, and left
His bed, and the warm rugs whereon he lay;   95
And o'er his chilly limbs his woollen coat
He passed, and tied his sandals on his feet,
And threw a white cloak round him, and he took
In his right hand a ruler's staff, no sword;
And on his head he set his sheep-skin cap,   100

Black, glossy, curled, the fleece of Kara-Kul;
And raised the curtain of his tent, and called
His herald to his side, and went abroad.
    The sun by this had risen and cleared the fog
From the broad Oxus and the glittering sands.   105
And from their tents the Tartar horsemen filed
Into the open plain; so Haman bade —
Haman, who next to Peran-Wisa ruled
The host, and still was in his lusty prime.
From their black tents, long files of horse, they
    streamed;   110
As when some grey November morn the files,
In marching order spread, of long-necked cranes
Stream over Casbin and the southern slopes
Of Elburz, from the Aralian estuaries,
Or some frore Caspian reed-bed, southward
    bound   115
For the warm Persian sea-board — so they streamed.
The Tartars of the Oxus, the King's guard,
First, with black sheep-skin caps and with long
    spears;
Large men, large steeds; who from Bokhara come
And Khiva, and ferment the milk of mares.   120
Next, the more temperate Toorkmuns of the south,
The Tukas, and the lances of Salore,
And those from Attruck and the Caspian sands;
Light men and on light steeds, who only drink
The acrid milk of camels, and their wells.   125
And then a swarm of wandering horse, who came
From far, and a more doubtful service owned;
The Tartars of Ferghana, from the banks
Of the Jaxartes, men with scanty beards
And close-set skull-caps; and those wilder
    hordes   130
Who roam o'er Kipchak and the northern waste,
Kalmuks and unkempt Kuzzaks, tribes who stray
Nearest the Pole, and wandering Kirghizzes,
Who come on shaggy ponies from Pamere,

These all filed out from camp into the plain.   135
And on the other side the Persians formed;
First a light cloud of horse, Tartars they seemed,
The Ilyats of Khorassan; and behind,
The royal troops of Persia, horse and foot,
Marshalled battalions bright in burnished steel.   140
But Peran-Wisa with his herald came,
Threading the Tartar squadrons to the front,
And with his staff kept back the foremost ranks.
And when Ferood, who led the Persians, saw
That Peran-Wisa kept the Tartars back,   145
He took his spear, and to the front he came,
And checked his ranks, and fixed them where they
    stood.
And the old Tartar came upon the sand
Betwixt the silent hosts, and spake, and said: —
    'Ferood, and ye, Persians and Tartars, hear!   150
Let there be truce between the hosts to-day.
But choose a champion from the Persian lords
To fight our champion Sohrab, man to man.'
    As, in the country, on a morn in June,
When the dew glistens on the pearlèd ears,   155
A shiver runs through the deep corn for joy —
So, when they heard what Peran-Wisa said,
A thrill through all the Tartar squadrons ran
Of pride and hope for Sohrab, whom they loved.
    But as a troop of pedlars, from Cabool,   160
Cross underneath the Indian Caucasus,
That vast sky-neighbouring mountain of milk snow;
Crossing so high, that, as they mount, they pass
Long flocks of travelling birds dead on the snow,
Choked by the air, and scarce can they
    themselves   165
Slake their parched throats with sugared
    mulberries —
In single file they move, and stop their breath,
For fear they should dislodge the o'erhanging
    snows —

So the pale Persians held their breath with fear.
And to Ferood his brother chiefs came up   170
To counsel; Gudurz and Zoarrah came,
And Feraburz, who ruled the Persian host
Second, and was the uncle of the King;
These came and counselled, and then Gudurz
    said: —
  'Ferood, shame bids us take their challenge up,   175
Yet champion have we none to match this youth.
He has the wild stag's foot, the lion's heart.
But Rustum came last night; aloof he sits
And sullen, and has pitched his tents apart.
Him will I seek, and carry to his ear   180
The Tartar challenge, and this young man's name.
Haply he will forget his wrath, and fight.
Stand forth the while, and take their challenge up.'
  So spake he; and Ferood stood forth and cried: —
'Old man, be it agreed as thou hast said!   185
Let Sohrab arm, and we will find a man.'
  He spake: and Peran-Wisa turned, and strode
Back through the opening squadrons to his tent.
But through the anxious Persians Gudurz ran,
And crossed the camp which lay behind, and
    reached,   190
Out on the sands beyond it, Rustum's tents.
Of scarlet cloth they were, and glittering gay,
Just pitched; the high pavilion in the midst
Was Rustum's, and his men lay camped around.
And Gudurz entered Rustum's tent, and found   195
Rustum; his morning meal was done, but still
The table stood before him, charged with food —
A side of roasted sheep, and cakes of bread,
And dark green melons; and there Rustum sate
Listless, and held a falcon on his wrist,   200
And played with it; but Gudurz came and stood
Before him; and he looked, and saw him stand,
And with a cry sprang up and dropped the bird,
And greeted Gudurz with both hands, and said: —

'Welcome! these eyes could see no better sight. 205
What news? but sit down first, and eat and drink.'
    But Gudurz stood in the tent-door, and said: —
'Not now! a time will come to eat and drink,
But not to-day; to-day has other needs.
The armies are drawn out, and stand at
        gaze;   210
For from the Tartars is a challenge brought
To pick a champion from the Persian lords
To fight their champion — and thou know'st his
        name —
Sohrab men call him, but his birth is hid.
O Rustum, like thy might is this young man's!   215
He has the wild stag's foot, the lion's heart;
And he is young, and Iran's chiefs are old,
Or else too weak; and all eyes turn to thee.
Come down and help us, Rustum, or we lose!'
    He spoke: but Rustum answered with a
        smile: —   220
'Go to! if Iran's chiefs are old, then I
Am older; if the young are weak, the King
Errs strangely; for the King, for Kai Khosroo,
Himself is young, and honours younger men,
And lets the agéd moulder to their graves.   225
Rustum he loves no more, but loves the young —
The young may rise at Sohrab's vaunts, not I.
For what care I, though all speak Sohrab's fame?
For would that I myself had such a son,
And not that one slight helpless girl I have —   230
A son so famed, so brave, to send to war,
And I to tarry with the snow-haired Zal,
My father, whom the robber Afghans vex,
And clip his borders short, and drive his herds,
And he has none to guard his weak old age.   235
There would I go, and hang my armour up,
And with my great name fence that weak old man,
And spend the goodly treasures I have got,
And rest my age, and hear of Sohrab's fame,

And leave to death the hosts of thankless kings,   240
And with these slaughterous hands draw sword
   no more.'
   He spoke, and smiled; and Gudurz made reply: —
'What then, O Rustum, will men say to this,
When Sohrab dares our bravest forth, and seeks
Thee most of all, and thou, whom most he seeks,   245
Hidest thy face? Take heed lest men should say:
Like some old miser, Rustum hoards his fame,
And shuns to peril it with younger men.'
   And, greatly moved, then Rustum made reply: —
'O Gudurz, wherefore dost thou say such
   words?   250
Thou knowest better words than this to say.
What is one more, one less, obscure or famed,
Valiant or craven, young or old, to me?
Are not they mortal, am not I myself?
But who for men of nought would do great
   deeds?   255
Come, thou shalt see how Rustum hoards his fame!
But I will fight unknown, and in plain arms;
Let not men say of Rustum, he was matched
In single fight with any mortal man.'
   He spoke, and frowned; and Gudurz turned,
   and ran   260
Back quickly through the camp in fear and joy —
Fear at his wrath, but joy that Rustum came.
But Rustum strode to his tent-door, and called
His followers in, and bade them bring his arms,
And clad himself in steel; the arms he chose   265
Were plain, and on his shield was no device,
Only his helm was rich, inlaid with gold,
And, from the fluted spine atop, a plume
Of horsehair waved, a scarlet horsehair plume.
So armed, he issued forth; and Ruksh, his horse, 270
Followed him like a faithful hound at heel —
Ruksh, whose renown was noised through all the
   earth,

The horse, whom Rustum on a foray once
Did in Bokhara by the river find
A colt beneath its dam, and drove him home,   275
And reared him; a bright bay, with lofty crest,
Dight with a saddle-cloth of broidered green
Crusted with gold, and on the ground were worked
All beasts of chase, all beasts which hunters know.
So followed, Rustum left his tents, and crossed   280
The camp, and to the Persian host appeared.
And all the Persians knew him, and with shouts
Hailed; but the Tartars knew not who he was.
And dear as the wet diver to the eyes
Of his pale wife who waits and weeps on shore,   285
By sandy Bahrein, in the Persian Gulf,
Plunging all day in the blue waves, at night,
Having made up his tale of precious pearls,
Rejoins her in their hut upon the sands —
So dear to the pale Persians Rustum came.   290
    And Rustum to the Persian front advanced,
And Sohrab armed in Haman's tent, and came.
And as afield the reapers cut a swath
Down through the middle of a rich man's corn,
And on each side are squares of standing corn,   295
And in the midst a stubble, short and bare —
So on each side were squares of men, with spears
Bristling, and in the midst, the open sand.
And Rustum came upon the sand, and cast
His eyes toward the Tartar tents, and saw   300
Sohrab come forth, and eyed him as he came.
    As some rich woman, on a winter's morn,
Eyes through her silken curtains the poor drudge
Who with numb blackened fingers makes her fire —
At cock-crow, on a starlit winter's morn,   305
When the frost flowers the whitened
    window-panes —
And wonders how she lives, and what the thoughts
Of that poor drudge may be; so Rustum eyed
The unknown adventurous youth, who from afar

Came seeking Rustum, and defying forth 310
All the most valiant chiefs; long he perused
His spirited air, and wondered who he was.
For very young he seemed, tenderly reared;
Like some young cypress, tall, and dark, and
   straight,
Which in a queen's secluded garden throws 315
Its slight dark shadow on the moonlit turf,
By midnight, to a bubbling fountain's sound —
So slender Sohrab seemed, so softly reared.
And a deep pity entered Rustum's soul
As he beheld him coming; and he stood, 320
And beckoned to him with his hand, and said: —
  'O thou young man, the air of Heaven is soft,
And warm, and pleasant; but the grave is cold!
Heaven's air is better than the cold dead grave.
Behold me! I am vast, and clad in iron, 325
And tried; and I have stood on many a field
Of blood, and I have fought with many a foe —
Never was that field lost, or that foe saved.
O Sohrab, wherefore wilt thou rush on death?
Be governed! quit the Tartar host, and come 330
To Iran, and be as my son to me,
And fight beneath my banner till I die!
There are no youths in Iran brave as thou.'
  So he spake, mildly; Sohrab heard his voice,
The mighty voice of Rustum, and he saw 335
His giant figure planted on the sand,
Sole, like some single tower, which a chief
Hath builded on the waste in former years
Against the robbers; and he saw that head,
Streaked with its first grey hairs; hope filled his
  soul,
                         340
And he ran forward and embraced his knees,
And clasped his hand within his own, and said: —
  'O, by thy father's head! by thine own soul!
Art thou not Rustum? speak! art thou not he?'
  But Rustum eyed askance the kneeling youth, 345

And turned away, and spake to his own soul: —
   'Ah me, I muse what this young fox may mean!
False, wily, boastful, are these Tartar boys.
For if I now confess this thing he asks,
And hide it not, but say: *Rustum is here!*   350
He will not yield indeed, nor quit our foes,
But he will find some pretext not to fight,
And praise my fame, and proffer courteous gifts,
A belt or sword perhaps, and go his way.
And on a feast-tide, in Afrasiab's hall,   355
In Samarcand, he will arise and cry:
"I challenged once, when the two armies camped
Beside the Oxus, all the Persian lords
To cope with me in single fight; but they
Shrank, only Rustum dared; then he and I   360
Changed gifts, and went on equal terms away."
So will he speak, perhaps, while men applaud;
Then were the chiefs of Iran shamed through me.'
   And then he turned, and sternly spake aloud: —
'Rise! wherefore dost thou vainly question thus   365
Of Rustum? I am here, whom thou hast called
By challenge forth; make good thy vaunt, or yield!
Is it with Rustum only thou wouldst fight?
Rash boy, men look on Rustum's face and flee!
For well I know, that did great Rustum stand   370
Before thy face this day, and were revealed,
There would be then no talk of fighting more.
But being what I am, I tell thee this —
Do thou record it in thine inmost soul:
Either thou shalt renounce thy vaunt and yield,   375
Or else thy bones shall strew this sand, till winds
Bleach them, or Oxus with his summer floods,
Oxus in summer wash them all away.'
   He spoke; and Sohrab answered, on his feet: —
'Art thou so fierce? Thou wilt not fright me so!   380
I am no girl, to be made pale by words.
Yet this thou hast said well, did Rustum stand
Here on this field, there were no fighting then.

But Rustum is far hence, and we stand here.
Begin! thou art more vast, more dread than I,   385
And thou art proved, I know, and I am young —
But yet success sways with the breath of Heaven.
And though thou thinkest that thou knowest sure
Thy victory, yet thou canst not surely know.
For we are all, like swimmers in the sea,   390
Poised on the top of a huge wave of fate,
Which hangs uncertain to which side to fall.
And whether it will heave us up to land,
Or whether it will roll us out to sea,
Back out to sea, to the deep waves of death,   395
We know not, and no search will make us know;
Only the event will teach us in its hour.'
     He spoke, and Rustum answered not, but hurled
His spear; down from the shoulder, down it came,
As on some partridge in the corn a hawk   400
That long has towered in the airy clouds
Drops like a plummet; Sohrab saw it come,
And sprang aside, quick as a flash; the spear
Hissed, and went quivering down into the sand,
Which it sent flying wide; then Sohrab threw   405
In turn, and full struck Rustum's shield; sharp rang,
The iron plates rang sharp, but turned the spear.
And Rustum seized his club, which none but he
Could wield; an unlopped trunk it was, and huge,
Still rough — like those which men in treeless
     plains   410
To build them boats fish from the flooded rivers,
Hyphasis or Hydaspes, when, high up
By their dark springs, the wind in winter-time
Hath made in Himalayan forests wrack,
And strewn the channels with torn boughs — so
     huge   415
The club which Rustum lifted now, and struck
One stroke; but again Sohrab sprang aside,
Lithe as the glancing snake, and the club came
Thundering to earth, and leapt from Rustum's hand.

And Rustum followed his own blow, and fell   420
To his knees, and with his fingers clutched the
   sand;
And now might Sohrab have unsheathed his sword,
And pierced the mighty Rustum while he lay
Dizzy, and on his knees, and choked with sand;
But he looked on, and smiled, nor bared his
   sword,   425
But courteously drew back, and spoke, and said: —
  'Thou strik'st too hard! that club of thine will float
Upon the summer-floods, and not my bones.
But rise, and be not wroth! not wroth am I;
No, when I see thee, wrath forsakes my soul.   430
Thou say'st, thou art not Rustum; be it so!
Who art thou then, that canst so touch my soul?
Boy as I am, I have seen battles too —
Have waded foremost in their bloody waves,
And heard their hollow roar of dying men;   435
But never was my heart thus touched before.
Are they from Heaven, these softenings of the heart?
O thou old warrior, let us yield to Heaven!
Come, plant we here in earth our angry spears,
And make a truce, and sit upon this sand,   440
And pledge each other in red wine, like friends,
And thou shalt talk to me of Rustum's deeds.
There are enough foes in the Persian host,
Whom I may meet, and strike, and feel no pang;
Champions enough Afrasiab has, whom thou   445
Mayst fight; *fight them*, when they confront thy
   spear!
But oh, let there be peace 'twixt thee and me!'
  He ceased, but while he spake, Rustum had risen,
And stood erect, trembling with rage; his club
He left to lie, but had regained his spear,   450
Whose fiery point now in his mailed right-hand
Blazed bright and baleful, like that autumn-star,
The baleful sign of fevers; dust had soiled
His stately crest, and dimmed his glittering arms.

His breast heaved, his lips foamed, and twice his
   voice   455
Was choked with rage; at last these words broke
   way: —
   'Girl! nimble with thy feet, not with thy hands!
Curled minion, dancer, coiner of sweet words!
Fight, let me hear thy hateful voice no more!
Thou art not in Afrasiab's gardens now   460
With Tartar girls, with whom thou art wont to
   dance;
But on the Oxus-sands, and in the dance
Of battle, and with me, who make no play
Of war; I fight it out, and hand to hand.
Speak not to me of truce, and pledge, and wine!   465
Remember all thy valour; try thy feints
And cunning! all the pity I had is gone;
Because thou hast shamed me before both the hosts
With thy light skipping tricks, and thy girl's wiles.'
   He spoke, and Sohrab kindled at his taunts,   470
And he too drew his sword; at once they rushed
Together, as two eagles on one prey
Come rushing down together from the clouds,
One from the east, one from the west; their shields
Dashed with a clang together, and a din   475
Rose, such as that the sinewy woodcutters
Make often in the forest's heart at morn,
Of hewing axes, crashing trees — such blows
Rustum and Sohrab on each other hailed.
And you would say that sun and stars took part   480
In that unnatural conflict: for a cloud
Grew suddenly in Heaven, and darked the sun
Over the fighters' heads; and a wind rose
Under their feet, and moaning swept the plain,
And in a sandy whirlwind wrapped the pair.   485
In gloom they twain were wrapped, and they alone;
For both the on-looking hosts on either hand
Stood in broad daylight, and the sky was pure,
And the sun sparkled on the Oxus stream.

But in the gloom they fought, with bloodshot
   eyes   490
And labouring breath; first Rustum struck the shield
Which Sohrab held stiff out; the steel-spiked spear
Rent the tough plates, but failed to reach the skin,
And Rustum plucked it back with angry groan.
Then Sohrab with his sword smote Rustum's
   helm,   495
Nor clove its steel quite through; but all the crest
He shore away, and that proud horsehair plume,
Never till now defiled, sank to the dust;
And Rustum bowed his head; but then the gloom
Grew blacker, thunder rumbled in the air,   500
And lightnings rent the cloud; and Ruksh, the horse,
Who stood at hand, uttered a dreadful cry;
No horse's cry was that, most like the roar
Of some pained desert-lion, who all day
Hath trailed the hunter's javelin in his side,   505
And comes at night to die upon the sand.
The two hosts heard that cry, and quaked for fear,
And Oxus curdled as it crossed his stream.
But Sohrab heard, and quailed not, but rushed on,
And struck again; and again Rustum bowed   510
His head; but this time all the blade, like glass,
Sprang in a thousand shivers on the helm,
And in the hand the hilt remained alone.
Then Rustum raised his head; his dreadful eyes
Glared, and he shook on high his menacing
   spear,   515
And shouted: *Rustum!* — Sohrab heard that shout,
And shrank amazed; back he recoiled one step,
And scanned with blinking eyes the advancing
   form;
And then he stood bewildered; and he dropped
His covering shield, and the spear pierced his
   side.   520
He reeled and staggering back, sank to the ground;
And then the gloom dispersed, and the wind fell,

And the bright sun broke forth, and melted all
The cloud; and the two armies saw the pair —
Saw Rustum standing, safe upon his feet,   525
And Sohrab, wounded, on the bloody sand.
 Then, with a bitter smile, Rustum began: —
'Sohrab, thou thoughtest in thy mind to kill
A Persian lord this day, and strip his corpse,
And bear thy trophies to Afrasiab's tent.   530
Or else that the great Rustum would come down
Himself to fight, and that thy wiles would move
His heart to take a gift, and let thee go.
And then that all the Tartar host would praise
Thy courage or thy craft, and spread thy fame,   535
To glad thy father in his weak old age.
Fool, thou art slain, and by an unknown man!
Dearer to the red jackals shalt thou be
Than to thy friends, and to thy father old.'
 And, with a fearless mien Sohrab replied: —   540
'Unknown thou art; yet thy fierce vaunt is vain.
Thou dost not slay me, proud and boastful man!
No! Rustum slays me, and this filial heart.
For were I matched with ten such men as thee,
And I were that which till to-day I was,   545
They should be lying here, I standing there.
But that belovèd name unnerved my arm —
That name, and something, I confess, in thee,
Which troubles all my heart, and made my shield
Fall; and thy spear transfixed an unarmed foe.   550
And now thou boastest, and insult'st my fate.
But hear thou this, fierce man, tremble to hear:
The mighty Rustum shall avenge my death!
My father, whom I seek through all the world,
He shall avenge my death, and punish thee!'   555
 As when some hunter in the spring hath found
A breeding eagle sitting on her nest,
Upon the craggy isle of a hill-lake,
And pierced her with an arrow as she rose,
And followed her to find her where she fell   560

Far off; anon her mate comes winging back
From hunting, and a great way off descries
His huddling young left sole; at that, he checks
His pinion, and with short uneasy sweeps
Circles above his eyry, with loud screams   565
Chiding his mate back to her nest; but she
Lies dying, with the arrow in her side,
In some far stony gorge out of his ken,
A heap of fluttering feathers — never more
Shall the lake glass her, flying over it;   570
Never the black and dripping precipices
Echo her stormy scream as she sails by —
As that poor bird flies home, nor knows his loss,
So Rustum knew not his own loss, but stood
Over his dying son, and knew him not.   575
    But, with a cold incredulous voice, he said: —
'What prate is this of fathers and revenge?
The mighty Rustum never had a son.'
    And, with a failing voice, Sohrab replied: —
'Ah yes, he had! and that lost son am I.   580
Surely the news will one day reach his ear,
Reach Rustum, where he sits, and tarries long,
Somewhere, I know not where, but far from here;
And pierce him like a stab, and make him leap
To arms, and cry for vengeance upon thee.   585
Fierce man, bethink thee, for an only son!
What will that grief, what will that vengeance be?
Oh, could I live, till I that grief had seen!
Yet him I pity not so much, but her,
My mother, who in Ader-baijan dwells   590
With that old king, her father, who grows grey
With age, and rules over the valiant Koords.
Her most I pity, who no more will see
Sohrab returning from the Tartar camp,
With spoils and honour, when the war is done.   595
But a dark rumour will be bruited up,
From tribe to tribe, until it reach her ear;
And then will that defenceless woman learn

That Sohrab will rejoice her sight no more,
But that in battle with a nameless foe,   600
By the far-distant Oxus, he is slain.'
He spoke; and as he ceased, he wept aloud,
Thinking of her he left, and his own death.
   He spoke; but Rustum listened, plunged in
    thought,
Nor did he yet believe it was his son   605
Who spoke, although he called back names he
   knew;
For he had had sure tidings that the babe,
Which was in Ader-baijan born to him,
Had been a puny girl, no boy at all —
So that sad mother sent him word, for fear   610
Rustum should seek the boy, to train in arms.
And so he deemed that either Sohrab took,
By a false boast, the style of Rustum's son;
Or that men gave it him, to swell his fame.
So deemed he; yet he listened, plunged in
   thought: 615
And his soul set to grief, as the vast tide
Of the bright rocking Ocean sets to shore
At the full moon; tears gathered in his eyes;
For he remembered his own early youth,
And all its bounding rapture; as, at dawn,   620
The shepherd from his mountain-lodge descries
A far, bright city, smitten by the sun,
Through many rolling clouds — so Rustum saw
His youth; saw Sohrab's mother, in her bloom;
And that old king, her father, who loved well   625
His wandering guest, and gave him his fair child
With joy; and all the pleasant life they led,
They three, in that long-distant summer-time —
The castle, and the dewy woods, and hunt
And hound, and morn on those delightful hills   630
In Ader-baijan. And he saw that Youth,
Of age and looks to be his own dear son,
Piteous and lovely, lying on the sand,

Like some rich hyacinth which by the scythe
Of an unskilful gardener has been cut,   635
Mowing the garden grass-plots near its bed,
And lies, a fragrant tower of purple bloom,
On the mown, dying grass — so Sohrab lay,
Lovely in death, upon the common sand.
And Rustum gazed on him with grief, and
      said: —   640
   'O Sohrab, thou indeed art such a son
Whom Rustum, wert thou his, might well have
      loved.
Yet here thou errest, Sohrab, or else men
Have told thee false — thou art not Rustum's son.
For Rustum had no son; one child he had —   645
But one — a girl; who with her mother now
Plies some light female task, nor dreams of us —
Of us she dreams not, nor of wounds, nor war.'
   But Sohrab answered him in wrath; for now
The anguish of the deep-fixed spear grew fierce,   650
And he desired to draw forth the steel,
And let the blood flow free, and so to die —
But first he would convince his stubborn foe;
And, rising sternly on one arm, he said: —
   'Man, who art thou who dost deny my words?   655
Truth sits upon the lips of dying men,
And falsehood, while I lived, was far from mine.
I tell thee, pricked upon this arm I bear
That seal which Rustum to my mother gave,
That she might prick it on the babe she bore.'   660
   He spoke; and all the blood left Rustum's cheeks,
And his knees tottered, and he smote his hand
Against his breast, his heavy mailèd hand,
That the hard iron corselet clanked aloud;
And to his heart he pressed the other hand   665
And in a hollow voice he spake, and said: —
   'Sohrab, that were a proof which could not lie!
If thou show this, then art thou Rustum's son.'
   Then, with weak hasty fingers, Sohrab loosed

His belt, and near the shoulder bared his arm, 670
And showed a sign in faint vermilion points
Pricked; as a cunning workman, in Pekin,
Pricks with vermilion some clear porcelain vase,
An emperor's gift — at early morn he paints,
And all day long, and, when night comes, the
    lamp 675
Lights up his studious forehead and thin hands —
So delicately pricked the sign appeared
On Sohrab's arm, the sign of Rustum's seal.
It was that griffin, which of old reared Zal,
Rustum's great father, whom they left to die, 680
A helpless babe, among the mountain-rocks;
Him that kind creature found, and reared, and
    loved —
Then Rustum took it for his glorious sign.
And Sohrab bared that image on his arm,
And himself scanned it long with mournful
    eyes, 685
And then he touched it with his hand and said: —
  'How say'st thou! Is that sign the proper sign
Of Rustum's son, or of some other man's?'
  He spoke; but Rustum gazed, and gazed, and
    stood
Speechless; and then he uttered one sharp cry: 690
O boy — thy father! — and his voice choked there.
And then a dark cloud passed before his eyes,
And his head swam, and he sank down to earth.
But Sohrab crawled to where he lay, and cast
His arms about his neck, and kissed his lips, 695
And with fond faltering fingers stroked his cheeks,
Trying to call him back to life; and life
Came back to Rustum, and he oped his eyes,
And they stood wide with horror; and he seized
In both his hands the dust which lay around, 700
And threw it on his head, and smirched his hair,
His hair, and face, and beard, and glittering arms;
And strong convulsive groanings shook his breast,

And his sobs choked him; and he clutched his
   sword,
To draw it, and for ever let life out.   705
But Sohrab saw his thought, and held his hands,
And with a soothing voice he spake, and said: —
   'Father, forbear! for I but meet to-day
The doom which at my birth was written down
In Heaven, and thou art Heaven's unconscious
   hand.   710
Surely my heart cried out that it was thou,
When first I saw thee; and thy heart spoke too,
I know it! but fate trod those promptings down
Under its iron heel; fate, fate engaged
The strife, and hurled me on my father's spear.   715
But let us speak no more of this! I find
My father; let me feel that I have found!
Come, sit beside me on this sand, and take
My head betwixt thy hands, and kiss my cheeks,
And wash them with thy tears, and say:
   My son!   720
Quick! quick! for numbered are my sands of life,
And swift; for like the lightning to this field
I came, and like the wind I go away —
Sudden, and swift, and like a passing wind.
But it was writ in Heaven that this should be.'   725
   So said he, and his voice released the heart
Of Rustum, and his tears broke forth; he cast
His arm around his son's neck, and wept aloud,
And kissed him. And awe fell on both the hosts,
When they saw Rustum's grief; and Ruksh, the
   horse,   730
With his head bowing to the ground and mane
Sweeping the dust, came near, and in mute woe
First to the one then to the other moved
His head, as if enquiring what their grief
Might mean; and from his dark, compassionate
   eyes,   735
The big warm tears rolled down, and caked the
   sand.

But Rustum chid him with stern voice, and said: —
   'Ruksh, now thou grievest; but, O Ruksh, thy feet
Should first have rotted on their nimble joints,
Or ere they brought thy master to this field!'   740
   But Sohrab looked upon the horse and said: —
'Is this, then, Ruksh? How often, in past days,
My mother told me of thee, thou brave steed,
My terrible father's terrible horse! and said,
That I should one day find thy lord and thee.   745
Come, let me lay my hand upon thy mane!
O Ruksh, thou art more fortunate than I;
For thou hast gone where I shall never go,
And snuffed the breezes of my father's home.
And thou hast trod the sands of Seistan,   750
And seen the River of Helmund, and the Lake
Of Zirrah; and the aged Zal himself
Has often stroked thy neck, and given thee food,
Corn in a golden platter soaked with wine,
And said: *O Ruksh! bear Rustum well!* — but I   755
Have never known my grandsire's furrowed face,
Nor seen his lofty house in Seistan,
Nor slaked my thirst at the clear Helmund stream;
But lodged among my father's foes, and seen
Afrasiab's cities only, Samarcand,   760
Bokhara, and lone Khiva in the waste,
And the black Toorkmun tents; and only drunk
The desert rivers, Moorghab and Tejend,
Kohik, and where the Kalmuks feed their sheep,
The northern Sir; and this great Oxus stream,   765
The yellow Oxus, by whose brink I die.'
   Then, with a heavy groan, Rustum bewailed: —
'Oh, that its waves were flowing over me!
Oh, that I saw its grains of yellow silt
Roll tumbling in the current o'er my head!'   770
   But, with a grave mild voice, Sohrab replied: —
'Desire not that, my father! thou must live.
For some are born to do great deeds, and live,
As some are born to be obscured, and die.

Do thou the deeds I die too young to do,   775
And reap a second glory in thine age;
Thou art my father, and thy gain is mine.
But come! thou seest this great host of men
Which follow me; I pray thee, slay not these!
Let me entreat for them; what have they done?   780
They followed me, my hope, my fame, my star.
Let them all cross the Oxus back in peace.
But me thou must bear hence, not send with them,
But carry me with thee to Seistan,
And place me on a bed, and mourn for me,   785
Thou, and the snow-haired Zal, and all thy friends.
And thou must lay me in that lovely earth,
And heap a stately mound above my bones,
And plant a far-seen pillar over all.
That so the passing horseman on the waste - 790
May see my tomb a great way off, and cry:
Sohrab, the mighty Rustum's son, lies there,
Whom his great father did in ignorance kill!
And I be not forgotten in my grave.'
  And, with a mournful voice, Rustum
  replied: —   795
'Fear not! as thou hast said, Sohrab, my son,
So shall it be; for I will burn my tents,
And quit the host, and bear thee hence with me,
And carry thee away to Seistan,
And place thee on a bed, and mourn for thee,   800
With the snow-headed Zal, and all my friends.
And I will lay thee in that lovely earth,
And heap a stately mound above thy bones,
And plant a far-seen pillar over all,
And men shall not forget thee in thy grave.   805
And I will spare thy host; yea, let them go!
Let them all cross the Oxus back in peace!
What should I do with slaying any more?
For would that all whom I have ever slain
Might be once more alive; my bitterest foes,   810
And they who were called champions in their time,
And through whose death I won that fame I have —

And I were nothing but a common man,
A poor, mean soldier, and without renown,
So thou mightest live too, my son, my son!   815
Or rather would that I, even I myself,
Might now be lying on this bloody sand,
Near death, and by an ignorant stroke of thine,
Not thou of mine! and I might die, not thou;
And I, not thou, be borne to Seistan;   820
And Zal might weep above my grave, not thine;
And say: *O son, I weep thee not too sore,*
For willingly, I know, thou met'st thine end!
But now in blood and battles was my youth,
And full of blood and battles is my age,   825
And I shall never end this life of blood.'
   Then, at the point of death, Sohrab replied: —
'A life of blood indeed, thou dreadful man!
But thou shalt yet have peace; only not now,
Not yet! but thou shalt have it on that day,   830
When thou shalt sail in a high-masted ship,
Thou and the other peers of Kai Khosroo,
Returning home over the salt blue sea,
From laying thy dear master in his grave.'
   And Rustum gazed in Sohrab's face, and
   said: —   835
'Soon be that day, my son, and deep that sea!
Till then, if fate so wills, let me endure.'
   He spoke; and Sohrab smiled on him, and took
The spear, and drew it from his side, and eased
His wound's imperious anguish; but the blood   840
Came welling from the open gash, and life
Flowed with the stream; all down his cold white
   side
The crimson torrent ran, dim now and soiled,
Like the soiled tissue of white violets
Left, freshly gathered, on their native bank,   845
By children whom their nurses call with haste
Indoors from the sun's eye; his head drooped low,
His limbs grew slack; motionless, white, he lay —

White, with eyes closed; only when heavy gasps,
Deep heavy gasps quivering through all his
   frame,   850
Convulsed him back to life, he opened them,
And fixed them feebly on his father's face;
Till now all strength was ebbed, and from his limbs
Unwillingly the spirit fled away,
Regretting the warm mansion which it left,   855
And youth, and bloom, and this delightful world.
  So, on the bloody sand, Sohrab lay dead;
And the great Rustum drew his horseman's cloak
Down o'er his face, and sate by his dead son.
As those black granite pillars, once high-reared   860
By Jemshid in Persepolis, to bear
His house, now 'mid their broken flights of steps
Lie prone, enormous, down the mountain side —
So in the sand lay Rustum by his son.
  And night came down over the solemn waste,   865
And the two gazing hosts, and that sole pair,
And darkened all; and a cold fog, with night,
Crept from the Oxus. Soon a hum arose,
As of a great assembly loosed, and fires
Began to twinkle through the fog; for now   870
Both armies moved to camp, and took their meal;
The Persians took it on the open sands
Southward, the Tartars by the river marge;
And Rustum and his son were left alone.
  But the majestic river floated on,   875
Out of the mist and hum of that low land,
Into the frosty starlight, and there moved,
Rejoicing, through the hushed Chorasmian waste,
Under the solitary moon; he flowed
Right for the polar star, past Orgunjè,   880
Brimming, and bright, and large; then sands begin
To hem his watery march, and dam his streams,
And split his currents; that for many a league
The shorn and parcelled Oxus strains along
Through beds of sand and matted rushy isles —   885

Oxus, forgetting the bright speed he had
In his high mountain-cradle in Pamere,
A foiled circuitous wanderer — till at last
The longed-for dash of waves is heard, and wide
His luminous home of waters opens, bright   890
And tranquil, from whose floor the new-bathed
    stars
Emerge, and shine upon the Aral Sea.

— Matthew Arnold

Glossary

Line

Line	Term	Meaning
2	Oxus	: a river flowing to the Aral sea
4	plunged in sleep	: sound sleep is contrasted with Sohrab's watchfulness.
5	Sohrab	: renowned warrior in single combat, commander of armies under Afrasiab's banners. Soon obtained a renown beyond all contemporary warriors but for his father Rustum.
	he	: a superfluous word, emphasises contrast
8	girt	: fastened his belt
11	Peran-Wisa	: Tartar general
16	strand	: part of river between low and high flow
23	laths	: thin strips of timber
38	King Afrasiab	: Tartar King
39	as thy son	: an ambiguous usage, meaning here 'as if I were your son'.
40	Samarcand	: a famous city of Turkestan
42	Ader-baijan	: a province of old Persia
45		: An example of Antithesis; a contrast shown through contrasting words used in succession

47	ensigns	: Sohrab hoists the Tartar flags over conquered lands
49	One man... one alone	:⎫ Examples of epic repetition
50-51	should greet, Should one day greet	:⎭ for the sake of emphasis
52	not unworthy, not inglorious	: the rhetorical figure of Litotes, a deliberate understatement [cf. 'a citizen of no mean city' ie., of a great city; 'he is no fool' ie., he is the reverse of fool.]
61	many names are sunk	: metaphorical for 'are lost', as a boat is lost when it sinks at sea
80	fray	: single combat
82	Seistan	: a region of Eastern Persia
88	fain would I know	: I would rather know
89	fain	: rather
91-92	but who can keep the lion's cub from ravening?	: rhetorical question equivalent to negative assertion
92	ravening	: voraciously devouring
101	Kara-Kul	: a district to the north of Oxus
103	herald abroad	: State proclamation-officer : out of his tent
107, 108	Haman	: army commander
111-116		: A characteristic simile of poet Homer. Here the comparison is between the Persian and Tartar armies to flocks of cranes
113	Casbin	: a city along Elburz mountain-range
115	frore	: frozen
119-120	Bokhara, Khiva	: districts of Central Asia
121-133		: Tartars, Toorkmuns, Tukas, Kalmuks, Kuzzaks, Khirgizzes – all nomadic tribes
122	lances	: a lance literally means a long wooden spear. Metonymy is the usage of the name of attribute or adjunct for that of the thing

		meant. Here lances is used to mean soldiers of the cavalry regiment armed with lances.
125	acrid	: strong
128	Ferghana	: a town in Central Asia
129	Jaxartes	: a river flowing into the Aral sea
130	hordes	: Tartar troops
138	Ilyats	: tribes
147	fixed	: stopped
150	Ferood	: royal Persian leader
160	Cabool	: Kabul, Afghan capital
171	Gudurz	: great Persian general
177	stag's foot	: nimble
	lion's heart	: courageous
178	Rustum	: the champion of the Persians, their one hope in single combat against Sohrab's challenge
182	wrath	: Rustum's anger against Persian King, and so would not fight for him
188	opening squadrons	: the troops made way
204	greeted ... hands	: Oriental way of greeting
221	go to	: an imperative expression of impatience
224 - 225	honours...graves	: Rustum carps against King Kai – Khosroo's preference for younger warriors
229	for would that I myself had such a son	: An instance of Dramatic Irony, a condition in which one seems to be mocked by fate or the facts
232	snow-haired	: hair white as snow
	Zal	: Rustum's father
237	fence	: defend
267	helm	: helmet
268	fluted	: grooved
	spine	: a metal spike
	plume	: feather-like crest

271	at heel	: close behind
272	Ruksh	: Rustum's famed horse, literally meaning 'lightning'
277	dight	: adorned
278	ground	: background
279	chase	: which go in pursuit
288	tale	: number
290	pale	: with suspense
293	swath	: a broad strip
296	stubble	: lower end of corn stalks
303	drudge	: slave
304	blackened	: with soot
305	cock-crow	: dawn
306	whitened	: with frozen moisture
310	defying	: challenging
311	perused	: examined carefully
328	field lost	: a usage of metonymy; the battle lost upon the field
345	eyed askance	: eyed with suspicion
347	fox	: cunning youth
355	feast-tide	: festive occasion
357 - 363		: Rustum's imagination of Sohrab's malign intention runs riot
375	vaunt	: boast
379	on his feet	: roused by the taunt
402	plummet	: weight attached to plumb-line
409	unlopped	: unstripped of branches and twigs
414	wrack	: wreck
418	lithe	: agile
	glancing	: darting
429	wroth	: angry
430	wrath	: anger
452	baleful	: deadly
458	curled	: with curly hair
	minion	: favourite child

466	feints	:	sham attacks
480-485		:	Pathetic Fallacy, ascribing human traits and feelings to inanimate nature
486	twain	:	two
499-501		:	another example of Pathetic Fallacy
507	quaked for	:	shook from fear
509	quailed not	:	did not shrink from fear
522	and then the gloom dispersed	:	when remedies are past griefs are ended
536	glad	:	gladden
540	mien	:	air, bearing
541	vaunt	:	boast
542	boastful man	:	connects boastful appearing in line 348
543	filial	:	adjective for son
557	breeding	:	bringing up
556-575	as when...him not	:	a simile dramatising Rustum's response to his horrendous blunder of slaying his own son
561	anon	:	soon
562	descries	:	sees
563	sole	:	alone
564	pinion	:	flight feathers
565	eyry	:	eagle's nest
568	gorge	:	steep part of a mountain
	ken	:	range of sight
570	glass her	:	reflect her image
590	mother	:	Tahmineh, daughter of King of Samengen
596	bruited up	:	voiced abroad
612-619		:	Rustum's emotions change to opposite direction as the wind upon tide
613	style	:	title
621	descries	:	discerns

632	of age	: of son's age
634	hyacinth	: plant with bell-shaped flowers
	scythe	: a garden implement
637	fragrant tower of purple bloom	: a famed towering personality with a regal bearing
653	would convince	: determined to convince
659	seal	: medallion used to make an imprint
664	corslet	: breast-plate, a piece of armour
	clanked	: heavy metallic sound
671	vermilion	: red
679	griffin	: a fabled creature with lion's body and eagle's head and wings
701	smirched	: soiled
706	thought	: suicidal intention
721	numbered are my sands of life	: I have but a short time to live. Comparison with hour-glass: fine sand passing from one bulb to another through a narrow neck in a definite time
750	Seistan	: town where Rustum's father Zal resides
751 - 765	Helmund, Moorghab, Tejend, Kohik, Sir	: names of rivers in Tartar territories and where campaigns took Sohrab. Helmund is in Afganistan, the rest are all in Turkestan
752	Zirrah	: name of a lake in Central Asia
754	platter	: dish, plate
756	furrowed	: wrinkled
766	yellow	: refers to the colour of sand in river Oxus
781	star	: fortune
789	far-seen	: seen a long way off
796 - 805		: another example of epic repetition; repetition for the sake of dignity to an epic poem (bear thee ... carry thee ... lay thee ... forget thee ...)

857 - 864		: an appropriate simile
861	Jemshid	: legendary Persian king noted as an example of human vanity. Said to have built the city of Persepolis, once the Persian empire's capital
	Persepolis	: in Persia (Iran) a place now noted for its ruins
865	waste	: refers to the battlefield, the Oxus banks
873	marge	: bank
878	Chorasmian	: name of a desert land at the lower end of the Oxus
880	right for the polar star	: due north
	Orgunjè	: a town on the Oxus
881	brimming	: flowing full
883	split	: ended his martial life
887	mountain-cradle in Pamere	: plateau in Pamera mountain
891	new bathed	: stars arising from the sea
875 - 892		: the poet hints that it is consoling that nature and life persist after sorrowful events. Time, akin to a flowing stream, washes away the pains of recollection.

The Tartars were at war with the Persians. At the time of this episode (circa 600 B.C.) Kai-Khosroo was the king of Persia. Rustum, the greatest warrior of the time, was the chief commander of his armies. Renowned for his strength and valour, he remained undefeated in single combat.

Rustum had married Tahmineh, daughter of the Turanian king of Samengan in Ader-baijan. He soon left her for the active life of war. A son, Sohrab, was born to them. However, Tahmineh sent word to Rustum that their issue was a daughter. She was afraid that her son would also be trained for war and exposed to the risk of death. Dejected by this news, Rustum never returned to his home.

Meanwhile, Sohrab grew up as a true son of his illustrious father with remarkable strength and skill in arms. He learnt of the glorious deeds of Rustum. Sohrab was determined to find his father and emulate his feats. Accordingly he set forth to wage war against Kai-Khosroo to conquer Persia and meet with his father.

Afrasiab, king of the Tartars, helped the young hero with an army and amenity to fight and destroy the mighty Rustum. Thus the king hoped to gain sovereignty over Persia as well. Afrasiab knew the relationship between Rustum and Sohrab but kept this crucial knowledge a secret. Thus, neither knew that they were father and son.

Rustum was terribly attached to the idea of possessing a son even before he had a child. His wife falsely informed him that the child born to them was a daughter. He was totally disappointed at the thought of not having a son to inherit his skill and valour. This dejection contributed to ending his active martial career. Against this backdrop, a triumphant Sohrab marched on to Persia and captured their strong frontier fortress. Having learnt of Sohrab's success, the alarmed Persian king sent for Rustum to come to his aid. With great difficulty Rustum was persuaded to fight his own unknown son in single combat. Rustum consented on the condition that he would fight incognito.

Rustum at first felt pity for Sohrab's youth. He proposed friendship instead of combat between them. Sohrab, thinking that his opponent's noble mien could only belong to his illustrious father, asked him if he were not indeed Rustum. Suspecting some trickery by the unknown youth, Rustum denied this. A terrible combat ensued.

During the course of the combat, the mighty Rustum charged at and missed the agile Sohrab and fell upon the sand. Leaving Sohrab the chance to unsheath his sword and pierce him. But Sohrab looked on, smiled and spoke to the unknown father. He pleaded if he could be hiding the fact that he was indeed Rustum. Rustum was enraged at the ignominy of being floored by the youngster, unprecedented as it was. He rose.

A fierce battle followed. The old warrior suddenly roared his own name, *Rustum!*, to inspire himself. Sohrab heard his father's name and shrank. That beloved name transfixed him. Bewildered and motionless, he dropped his protective shield. And Rustum pierced a defenceless Sohrab with his spear.

They taunted each other. It was a while before the pair realised their relationship. They were wonderstruck. A deluge of emotions engulfed them. Matthew Arnold magnificently captures their staggering sentiments. Rare indeed has literature portrayed such magnificent feelings in a human being.

The episode ends with the dying Sohrab prevailing upon Rustum to return to his mother. Sohrab had promised her that he would bring his father home. Having done his part, the son dies on the Oxus sands. The father returns home.

Infatuation spells disaster. Even before the birth of his son, Rustum was terribly attached to the idea of having a son. So was his wife attached to the son born to her. Sohrab himself was deeply attached to a father whom he had never met. With the result the father never enjoyed the company of the son. Neither did the son, the father's company. Their infatuation for one another produced only misery culminating in disaster.

The Fall of the Human Intellect
148 Pages

Stress, depression, disease in individuals and militancy, vandalism, terrorism in societies is threatening humanity with extinction. The book traces back the source of this impending disaster to the continual neglect of the human intellect. It highlights the fundamental difference between intelligence and intellect. Intelligence is acquired from schools and universities while the intellect is developed through one's personal effort in thinking, reasoning, questioning before accepting anything. The book is designed to develop the intellect and save humanity from self-destruction.

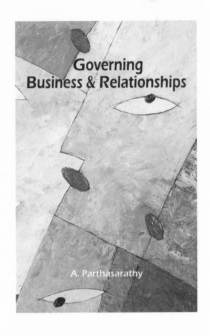

Governing Business & Relationships
203 Pages

Deals with the basic concepts associated with the running of a business such as Value Systems, Work Ethics, Stress Management, Productivity, Leadership and Time Management. Also analyses one's relationship with the world at large. The emphasis is on self development through study and reflection of the higher values of life rather than correcting the external world. Towards the end the book highlights a human being's role in achieving the ultimate management by gaining identity with one's own Self.

The Eternities: Vedanta Treatise
351 Pages

The book expounds the ancient philosophy of Vedanta. It presents the eternal principles of life and living. Living is a technique that needs to be learnt and practised by one and all. The technique provides the formula for remaining active all through life while maintaining inner peace. It helps one develop a powerful intellect to meet the challenges of the world.

Above all, the Treatise helps one evolve spiritually. It provides the knowledge and guidance to reach the ultimate in human perfection. The goal of Self-realisation.

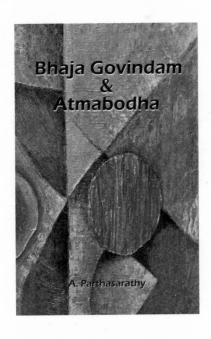

Bhaja Govindam & Atmabodha
232 Pages

Both the texts Bhaja Govindam and Atmabodha, were composed by Adi Shankaracharya in the eighth century. The Bhaja Govindam highlights the two human motivations – acquisition and enjoyment. Its thirty-one verses point out the delusion in external pursuit and urge one to seek the supreme Self. The Atmabodha is a picture gallery of word paintings in sixty-eight verses with deep philosophic themes. It contains several similes and metaphors taken from nature and life in general. The practical examples therein help a spiritual seeker to maintain the awareness of the supreme Reality in all walks of life.

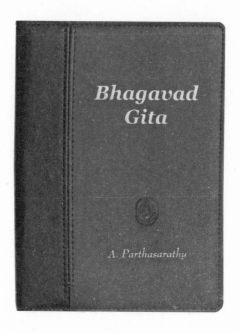

Bhagavad Gita
1080 Pages

The Gita brings to light the positive and negative tendencies that lie within you. They are your higher aspirations and lower desires in life that effect your evolution or devolution. Its chaste philosophy helps you conquer desire and regain the supreme Self. The state of Godhood. The book comprises the text, transliteration, word-meaning, translation and commentary. A useful contribution is the topic-wise division of each chapter which helps you capture the thought-flow and message therein.

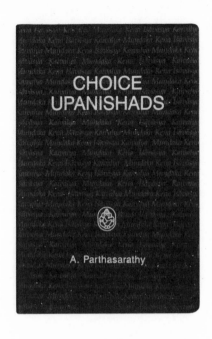

Choice Upanishads
243 Pages

The Upanishads form the final portion of the
Vedas which are considered the primeval source
of the scriptures. Sage Bādarāyaṇa Vyāsa classified
them as Rik, Sāma, Yajuh and Atharvana Vedas.
This book provides an exhaustive commentary
on four Upanishads namely Kena, Īśāvāsya,
Kaivalya and Muṇḍaka. The Upanishads
expound a system of philosophy which helps
humanity attain spiritual enlightenment.

The Symbolism of Hindu Gods and Rituals
183 Pages

A practical text explaining the allegorical
significance of gods and goddesses; rituals and
festivals; invocations and prayers. It educates a
spiritual aspirant on the philosophical aspect of
religious practices.

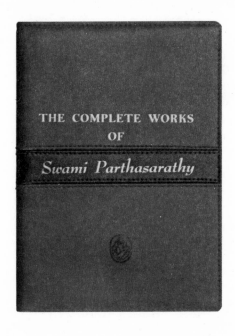

The Complete Works of Swami Parthasarathy
2532 Pages

The Complete Works of Swami Parthasarathy consists of:

1. The Fall of the Human Intellect

2. Governing Business & Relationships

3. Select English Poems

4. Vedanta Treatise: *The Eternities*

5. Bhaja Govindam & Atmabodha

6. Bhagavad Gita: 3 Volumes

7. Choice Upanishads

8. The Symbolism of Hindu Gods and Rituals

A. Parthasarathy is an internationally acclaimed philosopher with a multi-disciplined academic base including postgraduation from London University. He has researched for over sixty years on the state of human beings and focused on the urgent need to revive, rehabilitate the human intellect. His resolve has emerged into four distinct avenues of service:

Vedanta Academy
Parthasarathy founded the Academy in January 1988 in Malavli Hills, 108 kms from Mumbai, India. It offers three-year residential courses designed to build intellectual ability and instil higher values of life in students from India and abroad.

Public Discourses
His discourses on intellectual development have captivated audiences the world over for more than fifty years. And have been widely acclaimed by prestigious universities, institutions and organisations.

Corporate Seminars
He has been a distinguished resource of the Young Entrepreneur's Organisation (YEO), Young President's Organisation (YPO), World President's Organisation (WPO), World Economic Forum and several multinational corporations.

Writings
Parthasarathy has published ten books which present ancient philosophical teachings and wisdom of thinkers from the East and West. Three of them have earned bestselling status. These ten books have now been combined into a single volume entitled *The Complete Works of Swami Parthasarathy.*